Tapestry

Other books by Jelly Valimont

I Have Issues
Ghost writer for *Betrayed* by Randy Valimont

Tapestry

A STORY OF ADOPTION, ACCEPTANCE, & DESTINY

ARROWS &
STONES

For foreign and subsidiary rights, contact the author.

Cover design by: Leah Diaz Baty

ISBN: 978-1-957369-42-6   1 2 3 4 5 6 7 8 9 10

Printed in the United States of America

Dedication

To all adoptees who have ever felt the sting of rejection.

*To all adoptive families who took the chance on
a child that was not of their own blood.*

*To all birth families who, in unforeseen circumstances,
released a child to be loved by another.*

*May you all feel the truth of acceptance and
sense the destiny of God upon your life.*

This book is for you.

Contents

ACKNOWLEDGMENTS

In many ways, writing this book has been both a difficult endeavor and a somewhat therapeutic one. After we found Randy's birth family and began to see the intervention of God in Randy's life, Randy and I both knew that his story needed to be one that others heard. I just never envisioned that I would write this book without Randy by my side. However, I have heard his voice in my heart with every word I typed into the computer or often erased when he said, "No, you cannot put that in there!" Although he will never read my words, I am so very grateful for the forty-two years of love, life, and laughter that we shared. More than that, I am grateful to my heavenly Father who allowed us to share life and ministry. He has been my constant source of peace and comfort during the process of my grief.

I could have never continued with Tapestry had it not been for Randy's and my three daughters giving me a little push or a kick in the pants when I became overwhelmed. Jordan, you dreamed the magnitude of the project, helping me to not look at it as a list to be completed. Danielle, you offered ideas, reminding me of incidences that needed to be included, making me laugh at the memory. Alayna, you became my idea person, planning ways to expand the story so others would really know and understand your dad. You all exhibit different parts of your father's God-given gifts but operate individually within your own gifts from God.

To the Valimont family, I thank you from the depths of my heart for the part you played by becoming Randy's treasured family. Because of you, Randy became a man of God, wise beyond his years, loving and encouraging all who entered his life.

To the Boyles/Fotouhi families, I remain amazed by your love for Randy and our family, by your acceptance of the brother who could have been viewed as an embarrassment or a shame for you and your families. Thank you for embracing us and making us German/Iranians, or as Randy would say, "Ger-anians!"

To Griffin First Assembly, staff, board, members, and attendees, thank you for your continued love and support for our family during the most difficult time of our lives, for continuing to ask about the completion of the book, and for praying that God would direct me in His perfect path. We will never forget those who have stood with us and supported us in our time of grief.

To everyone else who entered Randy's life, impacted him, and helped him on his journey to acceptance of who he could become, I thank you, thank you, thank you.

Finally, thank you to Martijn van Tilborgh and your team for believing in this project enough to push it through to completion.

May God's blessings rest upon each and every one of you.

INTRODUCTION

DESIGNING A TAPESTRY

A tapestry is a rare type of art that was very common before the 20th century. It is not considered a fabric, a painting, or embroidery. It is a series of threads that are woven and tied onto other threads, creating a design or a beautiful picture.

There are many interesting things about tapestries that can relate to our lives. First, there must be a plan for weaving the tapestry. Second, the plan must be followed exactly, as if it were a mirror image or a blueprint of the work. When we are observing the designer at work, we may not know what the tapestry will be when it is finished. All we know is that something is being woven; it looks like a series of jumbled threads and could be anything when completed. The designer of the tapestry always has a master plan and knows what he or she is doing.

The threads of the tapestry must be gathered, the loom, which is the foundation, must be set in place, and the threads tied onto the loom to begin the process. It is then that the master weaver can begin to work. It is neither a quick process nor is it an easy one. Each thread is carefully chosen for a particular part of the design. The thread is woven into place and then tamped down repeatedly to provide a beautiful picture upon completion. It is only as time and work progress that the design will begin to make sense to those watching the process. For the one who is observing the back side or the "inside" of the process, the work seems to be a jumble of disconnected threads and knots. As progress is made, the disconnected threads provide an understandable, obvious design. A tapestry may take many years and many people to bring it to completion. It is a very intricate piece of art, needing many hands, many hours, days, weeks, and even years to finish.

|||||||||||||||||||||||||||||||||||||||||||||||||||||||||||||||||||||||||||||||||||

It is only as time and work progress that the tapestry's design will begin to make sense to those watching the process.

Our lives are much like a tapestry that has been designed by a master weaver. The foundation of your personal tapestry was set in place long before we were ever born. The threads in your tapestry are the people who have been placed intricately in your life to help produce a beautiful picture. Some threads may be placed in the picture for only a short time; while others may be woven throughout your entire life. Some may even be introduced into the tapestry later to add some richness to your life. These threads or people provide the color, the life, the picture, and the definition of what God is weaving in your particular tapestry. The threads in the picture that are pushed together or tamped down may represent experiences in your life and difficulties that cannot be explained and may never be understood. This process may be somewhat painful as all the threads are pushed and woven into place.

Simple designs take less time than complicated ones, as intricate and beautiful designs take more time and effort. It is not the actual picture that gives the tapestry its value. It is the time that it takes to get to the finished product. Amazingly, when the tapestry is finished, the back side of the tapestry is exactly like the front. It does not matter if you are looking at the front or the back of the tapestry, you will still understand the picture, the design that has been woven. What may have begun as a tangled jumble of threads and knots will, in the end, be a beautiful work of art.

In essence, your complicated, beautiful, intricate life will take much time and effort. God can design it to be beautiful both on the front side and the back, the beginning and the end. Regardless of how you see it now or when it is finished, God's design is always, always perfect.

||||||||||||||||||||||||||||||||||||||||||||||||||||||||||||||||||||||||||||||||||||||

> Regardless of how you see it now or when it is finished, God's design is always, always perfect.

You may be at an impasse in your life. You may be adopted or feel rejected, betrayed, or unworthy of anything God may want to do in your life. You may even feel that your life is in such a state that God can do nothing with you. No matter the state of your life, the circumstances that you have faced, either in or out of your control, God still has a design, a perfect plan to use you and your life tapestry to bring a beautiful work of art to completion. God can still use you.

CHAPTER 1

GATHERING MATERIALS

Stories have a divine starting place.

In 1957, Ewan MacColl wrote a song entitled "The First Time Ever I Saw Your Face." The lyrics of the song further state, "I thought the sun rose in your eyes, and the moon and the stars were the gifts you gave. . . ."[1] That is exactly how I felt the first time I ever saw Randy Valimont. It was a moment when I felt a decided shaking of my world. Not many people can state that they knew destiny was unfolding, but it seems that I did. It was not love at first sight, but there was a definite interest for both of us.

I was a second-semester freshman at Southeastern University, and Randy was just arriving for his first semester. I was standing in the cafeteria with my friends and a young man I was dating at the time when Randy walked in the door, stood there for a moment, and walked by us. I was laughing (loudly, I might add), and he flinched.

---

1 Roberta Flack, vocalist, "The First Time Ever I Saw Your Face," by Ewan MacColl, released June 30, 1975, track 6 on *First Take*, Atlantic Records.

We did not introduce ourselves, but I knew at that moment there was something special and unique about Randy Valimont.

As we became acquainted that semester, I labeled him a "player," and he labeled me "flirtatious." We neither dated nor did we know that we one day would, but I sensed that Randy had a strong call from God on his life. Randy was following God's call to be a minister. After being raised in a pastor's home, feeling the pressures, and seeing the pain of ministry, I never wanted to pursue a ministry call for my life. The last thing I wanted to do was date a young man who was pursuing what I was avoiding.

Randy's roommate that semester was Ron Crum, who, many years later, would become a part of our pastoral staff and would then become the senior pastor of Griffin First Assembly. Both Randy and Ron were known on campus as being "little preachers," devoted to the call on their lives. It was rare at that time to see two future pastors so devoted to their walk with the Lord, as many of our fellow students were not. Some were hypocritical and often played hurtful games in their relationships.

> Randy knew that God had called him to a task, and he would do nothing purposeful to forestall God's destiny for his life.

Randy did not belong in that category. He knew that God had called him to a task, and he would do nothing purposeful to forestall

God's destiny for his life. It was almost as if God had placed Randy and Ron together to help build their spiritual strength in a somewhat hostile and ungodly atmosphere. It also helped that they were both interested in enjoying life together.

Our social lives crossed often at athletic games and beaches in the area, but we were both dating other people and uninterested in a different relationship. The semester ended, and we went our separate ways, both of us using the summer to end our existing relationships.

I struggled that summer, thinking I would not return to college. I would get a job locally and volunteer in the local church. During that same time, Randy dug ditches for a local construction company, trying to make enough money to go back to college and pleading for God to use him. We later determined that, for both of us, our own desires and wishes were not as strong as the desire to find the will of God for our lives. As we both prayed to determine our next steps, God intervened in my heart and in Randy's finances, and we both returned to college for another year, never knowing what was unfolding in our life plan.

I did not know that God was already weaving a tapestry of destiny for our lives together. He would give us a beautiful rendition of His love and grace before He was finished.

The steps to making a tapestry are completed in a certain order. Too often we begin our own projects, never knowing what we are doing, where we are going, or how we will get there. We start something without counting the cost. Maybe we think we understand the cost but find that there are always cost overruns.

Just as an experienced builder would never begin building a structure without a blueprint, a truly experienced weaver would never begin a project with no idea of how the finished project would appear. A successfully created tapestry of significance is never a hap-hazard, jumbled, half-idealized project. Similarly, in our lives, some things occur during the weaving process that are uncontrollable, cannot be foreseen, or are added by mistake, due to someone not following the master plan.

Once the tapestry is begun, the experienced weaver knows exactly how to bring the project to completion but may not share that process with those who are observing. The experienced weaver will not explain to the tapestry what he, the master weaver, is doing. He will not say, "Just wait until I am finished, and you will be beautiful!" He may place a thread on one side and move it into position, causing it to look as if it is totally out of place, while another unused thread may look as if it would fit perfectly. However, as the project continues, the picture emerges, and understanding dawns.

|||||||||||||||||||||||||||||||||||||||||||||||||||||||||||||||||||||||||||||||||||||||||

> The experienced weaver will not explain to the tapestry what he, the master weaver, is doing. He will not say, "Just wait until I am finished, and you will be beautiful!"

All our stories have a divine starting place and divine intervention. Randy's story began in 1959 with his conception. God divinely intervened to ensure that his life would be completed to be a beautiful tapestry of God's grace on his life. God was the master weaver and knew exactly what He wanted to do with Randy's life. There were times when the threads of his life looked out of place and impractical, but we eventually saw his life story emerging. We did not know what God was doing because we could not see the finished project. We learned to trust God's hand in our lives and to wait until God finished that part of the picture before we tried to unravel what was done. While we may have thought that a certain thread did not belong, that it needed to be unraveled and begun again, God had a plan and a design in place that we did not understand. It was only toward the end of Randy's life that the picture began to emerge, and we had some understanding of what God had truly done.

God is a holy God. There is no wickedness or unholiness in Him. He does not bring temptation or sin into our lives. We have a free will, and when we are tempted to sin, we can choose the direction for our lives. Will we choose righteousness or sinfulness? It was not in God's divine plan that an affair would result in Randy's conception. It was not in God's plan for hurt, heartache, rejection, and betrayal to occur, but He used what happened. When God's primary plan is interrupted, He has an alternate plan waiting to ensure that the tapestry He designed will be completed.

Just as a tapestry has a plan and a design, there comes a time when the master weaver will pronounce that the tapestry—the life—is finished. Whether we are doing a project, going on a journey, developing a life plan, or getting an education, we begin and end, start and stop, somewhere. In fact, the very first scripture in the Word of God states, "In the beginning, God. . . ." God put in us the desire to have an understanding of the beginning and to sometimes look forward to the end.

Because we are finite creatures, we operate in beginnings and endings, especially when considering life. Our lives begin somewhere, at some time. Parents will often mark the beginning of our lives with a birthday. We then live our lives, hopefully, to the best of our abilities and accomplish all we choose to do, all that God has called us to do. Then, at some point in time, our lives will end. If we are fortunate to live long lives, we look back, reflect, and wonder if we did all we could have, if we have used everything God put in us, and if we are leaving a legacy—something that will affect generations to come.

Some of us are fortunate enough to know that our parents loved us, and we were conceived in that love. Others are not so fortunate. When we know that our parents love us, that knowledge gives us a secure foundation on which to build our lives. When we are unsure of that love, don't know if our parents loved each other, loved us, or were happy they had conceived a child, then our foundation, the beginning of our lives, is not as stable or secure. In addition, whenever a child is adopted, that child may struggle with a greater sense of trying to understand their beginning. The parents of that adopted child may constantly reaffirm their love for the child but be unable to provide the answers and the security that child needs.

IIIIIIIIIIIIIIIIIIIIIIIIIIIIIIIIIIIIIIIIIIIIIIIIIIIIIIIIIIIIIIIIIIIIIIIIIIIIIIIIIIII

Some of us are fortunate enough
to know that our parents loved
us, and we were conceived in that
love. Others are not so fortunate.

According to Dr. Allan N. Schwarz, PhD, many children who are adopted will face psychological issues in life.[2] Some will feel rejected and abandoned while others will feel low self-esteem.[3] In fact, evidence exists that babies may sense while in the womb if they are wanted or celebrated. Some refer to this as "rejection syndrome" or "adopted child syndrome." This is not necessarily a result of good or bad parenting but a result of the struggle for self-identity. *Who am I? Where did I come from? What am I supposed to do in life? Am I loved? Am I significant?*

Although he did not want to meet his birth parents or know the entire story when he was a young man, Randy did have many questions about the beginning of his life. He made assumptions and answered the questions in his heart to the best of his ability. He looked for people who looked like him, thought like him, and had the same ideas. It was only later in his life that the questions in his heart were answered in ways he could have never envisioned.

The story you are reading is the story of one baby, Randy Valimont, whose life began with rejection. However, that is not the end of the story. It is also the story of how rejection became adoption, how Randy accepted that adoption, and, ultimately, how he saw part of his destiny fulfilled.

---

2 Allan N. Schwartz, PhD, "Long-Term Issues for the Adopted Child," *Mental Help*, www.mentalhelp.net/parenting/long-term-issues-for-the-adopted-child/.

3 Allan N. Schwartz, PhD, "Psychological Issues Faced by Adopted Children and Adults." *Mental Help*, www.mentalhelp.net/parenting/psychological-issues-faced-by-adopted-children-and-adults/.

CHAPTER 2

ADOPTION

The design, the loom, and the threads are put into place.

THREADS OF THE TAPESTRY

June and Norman's Story

June was a young girl when her father, a Russian immigrant, came to know Jesus Christ and left the Greek Orthodox church. Ray Lukensow was raised in an abrasive home and was, in turn, rearing his six children in the same manner. When Christ came into their lives, He not only eternally changed Ray, but Christ changed the atmosphere of the home. The love of Christ began to permeate the home and be displayed throughout their lives. As a result of her father's salvation and their subsequent attendance at the local church, June accepted Christ as her Savior and began to feel that her destiny was to follow Christ as a missionary. She answered the call with a resounding "Yes!" and began to prepare for her training in missions.

One of the first steps that June took to fulfill her call was to attend Bible school at Elam Bible Institute. There, she met a young man who she thought would be her future husband, and they made plans to follow Christ onto the mission field. After a few short months of preparation, June became ill, requiring her to return home for medical testing and to recover her health. June's doctors found that some of the kidney issues with which she had been plagued her entire life had come about because both kidneys were on the same side of her body. Only one kidney was functional. At that time, there was nothing that medical science could do for her except to make her comfortable and hope that her issues did not worsen.

June spent a few months recuperating and then returned to school. She knew that her diagnosis might affect her future as a missionary; however, she was also sure that she and her fiancé would give everything to remain in the Lord's work. As she continued with her studies, her fiancé told her that in her absence, he had fallen in love with someone else. Her engagement was at an end. Her hopes and dreams for missions work and ministry with him were dashed. She left school as a disappointed young woman, wondering if she had been mistaken. Did God have work for her to do in missions? Had He called her to ministry?

June resumed life at home in New York and met and married a man who would ultimately encourage her in her life work. This set in motion the events that still affect thousands today: June was unable to follow the call of God into missions work, but God would eventually allow her child to not only go to more than sixty nations of the world to preach the gospel, but he would also raise millions of dollars for the cause of missions both domestic and foreign.

June Lukensow and Norman Valimont married on September 5, 1953, eager to begin their family together. Although God did not call Norman into ministry, he was a good man, intent on providing for his family and working hard to do so. Unfortunately, many months passed without any signs of children being added to the new Valimont family.

||||||||||||||||||||||||||||||||||||||||||||||||||||||||||||||||||||||||||||||||||

> Had June missed God? Had she never heard from Him? Had God abandoned her? Did He love and care for her? Why had God allowed this to happen?

Months turned into years, and June never conceived. She returned to the doctors and was devastated to learn that she would never bear children due to her continued kidney problems and other previously undiagnosed physical issues. She had come from a large family and had just assumed that she would, one day, have children. Her dreams had again been thwarted, and she questioned the plan of God in her life. Had she missed God? Had she never heard from Him? Had God abandoned her? Did He love and care for her? Why had God allowed this to happen? She had been pronounced a barren woman, never to bear children or see the fulfillment of her dreams. Her physical condition alone was enough to cause consternation, but adding the devastating news of barrenness was more than she could bear. Circumstances beyond her control again broke June's heart.

After learning that she would never bear a biological child, June and Norman began the process of adopting a child or children who would complete their family. It was 1959. Adoption was not celebrated. It carried a social stigma for the child who was adopted—sometimes for both the adoptive parent and the adopted child. Often, the child was labeled "illegitimate" or a bastard and carried that stigma throughout life. As a result, many adoptive parents kept the process a secret from the child who was adopted so that society would not label them. Many children did not know they were adopted until later in life, often finding out by mistake.

Months passed for the Valimont couple before the adoption agency notified June and Norman that a baby girl was available. The birth mother had a few days to make a final decision, and during that time, the baby had been placed into social services, awaiting final placement. June and Norman returned home to prepare for their new baby girl. Furniture and gifts began to arrive in preparation. Finally, the day came for June and Norman to return to Pennsylvania to pick up their baby daughter. They arrived in great anticipation but left devastated upon being told that the birth mother had changed her mind and would be keeping the infant. They never knew what happened to the baby, if the mother had really chosen to keep her or if someone else had been given the baby girl they so desperately loved and wanted. The subsequent years never brought answers to the questions in their hearts.

June and Norman were disappointed and unsure of their next steps. We can all relate to similar heartache and remember times when we have felt those emotions. We may not have faced the same circumstances, but we've faced things that were beyond our under-standing and our comprehension. However, disappointment and devastation do not have to destroy us. They can point us, without our knowledge, and sometimes unwillingly, toward our destiny.

June could not easily embrace her destiny and wept profusely with her heartache. She began to pray through her pain and made a promise to God. She prayed a true "Hannah prayer," promising God that if He gave her children, she would give them back to Him.

The Bible, in 1 Samuel 1, says Hannah was the first wife of Elkanah. She was also a barren woman. Although Elkanah's second wife had children, Hannah did not. To make matters worse, the second wife harassed Hannah and made fun of her because of her barrenness. Hannah went to the temple every year with her husband and the rest of the family, but on one trip, her heart broken, Hannah fell on her face before God and prayed what has become known as the "Hannah Prayer":

> *Crushed in soul, Hannah prayed to God and cried*
> *and cried—inconsolably. Then she made a vow:*
> *"Oh, God-of-the-Angel-Armies,*
> *If you'll take a good, hard look at my pain,*
> *If you'll quit neglecting me and go into action for me*
> *By giving me a son,*
> *I'll give him completely, unreservedly to you.*
> *I'll set him apart for a life of holy discipline."*
> —1 Samuel 1:10-11 (MSG)

June never wavered in that promise. God looked into the heart of a devastated woman, and, knowing that her prayer was sincere, provided a thread of destiny in another tapestry that He would choose to weave.

||||||||||||||||||||||||||||||||||||||||||||||||||||||||||||||||||||||||||||||||

> God looked into the heart of a devastated woman, and, knowing that her prayer was sincere, provided a thread of destiny in another tapestry that He would choose to weave.

JOEL S'S STORY

Joel S., attorney-at-law, wanted a baby boy. Many couples on his adoption list had already been approved as potential acceptable parents. He and his wife were also on that list. He specialized in adoptions and knew that, eventually, someone would give birth to a baby boy that would be available for him to adopt. Two women were ready to deliver and give their babies—one a girl and one a boy—up for adoption. He began to anticipate that he and his wife would finally have a baby boy to call their own.

Then a broken young couple walked into his office on a tranquil afternoon, telling a devastating story of love and loss. June and Norman had done nothing wrong. The adoption of their baby girl had been thwarted either by an unscrupulous social worker or an indecisive, immature mother. The process was wrong and flawed, and Joel felt it necessary to right the wrong that had been done to them.

As the Valimont couple told him their story, he made a promise to them. Due to the circumstances, the next baby that became available for adoption would be theirs. They would not have to wait the required months or years it usually took to get a baby. They would not even have to go through another home visit or approval to be declared fit parents. He would see that they had a baby, and the process would move quickly. Although it would be a private adoption, the baby, upon reaching adulthood, could be given answers about his or her birth family.

Little did Joel S. know that he was providing another thread in a tapestry woven by God. What appeared to be a coincidence—a chance encounter—was the hand of God orchestrating a plan, a design that He wanted to complete. The work had already begun, and God would see it through to its ultimately beautiful end . . . a tapestry that would be a wonder to behold!

||||||||||||||||||||||||||||||||||||||||||||||||||||||||||||||||||||||||||||||||||||||||

The work had already begun,
and God would see it through
to its ultimately beautiful
end . . . a tapestry that would
be a wonder to behold!

MARION'S STORY

Marion was young, beautiful, and married. She had already given birth to four children. She and her husband had issues, and she felt trapped. As it became necessary for her to help support their growing family, Marion went to work as a secretary at the local hospital. It was a demanding job, but she was capable, and the hours were good. Her husband worked long hours too, and the job enabled her to get home early enough to take care of the children after school and prepare dinner for them.

While working at the hospital, she met a handsome young doctor who had just arrived from Iran. He was everything her husband was not, or at least that was the way she saw it at the time. His first language was Farsi, so his accent was both unusual and appealing. Parviz was complimentary, soft-spoken, educated, handsome, and lonely. He had left his wife and son in Iran to come to the United States and practice medicine. One day, depending on the circumstances, his family might follow him to the United States.

Although Marion had been raised in a Christian home and knew right from wrong, she and Parviz began to have an affair. Eventually, Marion's husband discovered the affair, and her marriage was shaken as never before. Marion and her husband separated while the affair between Marion and Parviz continued.

I do not know when the affair began, but someone told me that Marion became pregnant more than once and that she and Parviz decided that he would abort the babies. It was illegal at that time, so they had to hide both the pregnancies and the abortions. (The truth behind this is unknown as both Marion and Parviz are already in eternity.)

In 1959, Parviz's father summoned him to Iran to perform surgery on the wife of the Shah of Iran. Parviz and his family were close relatives of the Shah, and only those who were related could be trusted to perform medical procedures on the royal family. During his time away from the United States, Marion found that she was once again pregnant with a child belonging to Parviz. By the time Parviz returned to the United States, Marion was too advanced in her pregnancy for Parviz to abort the baby.

In addition to this dilemma, Marion realized that Parviz would not divorce his wife and marry her. She knew that she needed to return to her husband, ask forgiveness for her unfaithfulness, and restore their relationship. She did this, but one of the conditions to their reconciliation was that she gave up the baby that she carried. This baby was not her husband's child, and he had no desire to raise a child that did not belong to him.

I cannot know the condition of Marion's heart, nor can I understand how she could ever contemplate giving up a child. I only know that she had given birth to four other children and intimately knew the bond between a mother and her child—how a mother loves her children. To consider handing a child to someone and never knowing the life that child would lead must have been one of the greatest heartaches in her life. However, it was the condition for her marriage to be restored.

Marion carried and delivered the baby boy with no complications. All her earlier deliveries had been late by two to three weeks. For some reason, this delivery was early and uneventful. Those who attended to her during the delivery were aware that this one was different. There was no joy and excitement, no anticipation to see the newborn. Marion would not hold or feed the baby while she recovered at the hospital days after the delivery.

Due to her standing in the community and knowing people in the hospital, Marion could not just walk away from the baby. She would have to take the baby from the hospital to the attorney's office and give him away. Although this was long before local and federal privacy laws were enacted, Marion depended on the nurses and doctors in the hospital to not share what she saw as her shameful secret.

As the day arrived for Marion to leave the hospital and take the baby away, she asked the nurses to cover his face with a blanket. Marion held him in her arms, smelling that sweet baby smell, but could not look at his face. She later stated that she knew if she ever saw his face that she would not be able to give him to the attorney and the waiting adoptive family. By not seeing his face, she would never have to remember the child that she did not keep, the child who was evidence of her unfaithfulness to her marriage vows.

Marion and her husband left the hospital and drove immediately to Joel S's office. The attorney knew she was coming and had already informed the new adoptive parents, who were waiting in a private room. The attorney, June, Norman, and the birth mother signed the paperwork, making the adoption legal and final. The baby boy was surrendered to the attorney, who took him to the waiting couple. June and Norman Valimont now held their new son in their arms. It could have still fallen apart; they could have still walked away childless. They prayed that history would not be repeated and that they would leave the office with a new son.

As Joel S. handed the baby to June, she noticed that the baby's face was covered. She immediately took the blanket away from his face. She was the first mother to look at his face . . . kiss his chubby cheeks . . . and fall in love with him. She was the first mother to truly know that God had destined her to be a part of His predetermined plan to weave a life and a tapestry, to teach this baby to walk in the paths of a righteous man. She was part of God's design. As she began to see some of God's plan unfold before her eyes, she somewhat understood her previous disappointments and heartache.

||||||||||||||||||||||||||||||||||||||||||||||||||||||||||||||||||||||||||||||||||||||||||

As June began to see some of God's plan unfold before her eyes, she somewhat understood her previous disappointments and heartache.

Thus, God put another thread into place in the tapestry that He was weaving.

PARVIZ'S STORY

Parviz was born into the high society of Iran. His father was married to one woman but also had a concubine. Both relationships bore many children, and they were raised together in the same compound as one family. They were of Muslim descent, and this was an acceptable practice for their religion and their society.

As Parviz grew into a young man, his father, a local sheik, recognized the political upheaval that was headed for Iran. He knew that, due to political pressures, their lives would change one day, and they would possibly lose their livelihood. With some urging from the Shah and the United States government, his father made the decision to begin sending his children throughout the world to make their way, not dependent on family wealth or connections. Parviz was sent to the United States of America. They sent his siblings to various other countries.

When Parviz left Iran, he never planned to stay away. He left his wife and young son, fully intending to return and continue building his life in his home country. He and his family were close relatives of the Shah of Iran, and they would nurture that relationship as long as possible. While in Iran, they would dine and socialize at the palace regularly—sometimes up to four times a week.

While in America, Parviz was lonely and wanted the companionship of a woman and family to fill his time. He found the companionship he longed for with Marion and her children, never planning to make it a permanent relationship. He made no promises to Marion and was only fulfilling what was acceptable in his home country and in his culture. He saw no wrong in this.

At some point in 1959, the government called Parviz back to Iran to perform surgery on the wife of the Shah. He quickly went, never knowing that Marion had conceived a child and that when he returned to the United States, it would be far too late to perform another abortion. According to Marion, when he returned to the United States, he wanted nothing to do with the child. He also would never acknowledge that he was the father. This signaled the end of the affair with Marion and the restoration of her marriage. Parviz never saw the baby that he and Marion had conceived and never planned for this baby to be a part of his life or the life of his family. His wife probably never knew that Parviz had another son. (In addition, later information suggested that Parviz either did not know about the child or did not believe the child was his. Since all parties are deceased, I cannot confirm the information.)

Over the next few years, Parviz traveled between the United States and Iran, building his life and reputation as a surgeon. His skills earned him a position in Iran that is the equivalent of the surgeon general of the United States. He also built a local hospital where he treated the people of his country.

Political pressures continued to increase, and life became difficult for the family. Parviz's father, now a very powerful sheik, bowed to political pressures. At the request of the Shah, he agreed to give the family vineyards and orchards to the local people. He kept only a small part of the family property for himself and his family. He hoped that this would show his support to the Shah. While it may have shown his support, it also decimated the village economy as the local people knew little about cultivating and maintaining the orchards and vineyards. Their lack of knowledge resulted in a lower crop yield, sales, and income for the people. The people became restless and unhappy, giving the opportunity for more political upheaval to occur.

Parviz decided it was time for his family and him to emigrate to the United States and make it their home. He, his wife, son, and new daughter eventually relocated to the United States.

While Parviz may have wanted to fill his loneliness and follow the example of the multiple relationships of his Muslim father, his actions marked a course for destiny in the life of a child conceived from that unsanctioned relationship. He became a thread in the tapestry that God was weaving, a destiny that would be fulfilled.

|||||||||||||||||||||||||||||||||||||||||||||||||||||||||||||||||||||||||||||||||||||||

Parviz became a thread in the tapestry that God was weaving, a destiny that would be fulfilled.

CHAPTER 3

UNDERSTANDING, COPING, AND MAKING IT THROUGH THE PROCESS

The weaving and tamping continue.

LIFE IN NEW YORK

Randy knew that he was adopted. From his earliest recollections, the word was used freely and often. It was never hidden or spoken in hushed tones but was common knowledge in the family and the community. Adopted. As a young child, he didn't know what it meant, only that he was different. His mom told him that he did not come out of her belly, but he came from her heart. There was never any shame attached to the word "adoption" or any shame demonstrated by the family. Most of the extended family made Randy feel that he was even more unique because he was *chosen* to be a part of their family. One family member even confided to Randy that a family is stuck with those who are born into it, but the adopted ones are very special because they are chosen.

When he started school, Randy began to understand that not everyone had the same opinion about adoption or thought it was significant that he did not belong by blood to his family. As he got older and asked questions, June and Norman would answer only what they could: His parents were told that he was part Italian. It was a private adoption, not handled by a public agency but by a private attorney. It was also an open adoption which meant his birth records were not sealed. According to the terms of the adoption, after he became an adult, he could discover more information by contacting the department of vital records in Albany or the attorney who handled the adoption. It would be a very simple process. Randy knew the information was his for the asking throughout his life, but he did not want to ask.

At this time, the nation's culture did not accept adoption as honorable. If a woman could not bear a child, there was something gravely wrong with her. She often felt guilt and pain for being "less than a woman" or felt that she was somewhat flawed. If a child was given up for adoption, it was assumed there was something wrong with that child, he or she was less than perfect, or the child was "illegitimate." That simply meant that the parents were not married to one another when the child was born. Not only was this considered sinful, but being illegitimate also placed a stigma on that child for much of his or her life. Most legal documents at that time asked about parentage. When the question could not be answered or was left blank, the child often felt inadequate.

In addition, if a person could not document their parentage, they became known as a "bastard" child. People spoke of the child as being born "on the wrong side of the blanket," not good enough to integrate into society, or not good enough to be part of a family. As the child grew, parentage was often called into question, and speculation ran rampant. In the eyes of many, an illegitimate child or a child who did not know their ancestry was not a good candidate for marriage.

Randy was born on June 8, 1960, in Johnson City, New York. Within two months of his adoption, as so often happens, his once barren mother became pregnant with her first biological child, a son they named Jeff. Randy and Jeff were very close in age, at times very similar in size, and June often dressed them alike as twins. June and Norman had two miracles, both given to them by God's miraculous hand and destined to belong to Him.

June was determined to keep her promise to God that these children would belong to Him. She poured God's Word into their hearts every day of their lives. She prayed over them and spoke blessings of life and success into their spirits. Before they began their activities for the day, June would read a chapter from the book of Proverbs to them, incorporating wisdom into their hearts. It is a wonder how she could get those two little boys to sit still long enough to read an entire chapter to them! Regardless, as the boys grew, it became obvious that she had instilled the Word of God into them, and they were significantly affected by that wisdom.

||||||||||||||||||||||||||||||||||||||||||||||||||||||||||||||||||||||||||||||||||

June poured God's Word into their
hearts every day of their lives.

Randy's mischievous personality began to develop in those early years. One morning, he climbed into the bed with June, ready to start his day. He looked into her eyes, put both hands on her cheeks, and succinctly stated, "Mommy, if you won't aggabate me today, I won't aggabate you!" Having two boys so close in age and size must have been quite a challenge to her peace of mind!

In 1965, Randy began his kindergarten year of school and had a good and uneventful year. Randy was an intelligent student who showed much promise in academics. When he started first grade and his younger brother began kindergarten, school life changed for Randy. It was obvious that they didn't look alike and that their personalities were extremely different. To other students, Randy was not Jeff's "real" brother because he was adopted. Randy became known among his peers as the "bastard" because he didn't have a real dad and mom. I do not know who first used the word to describe Randy, but it became a word that was used frequently in relation to him in those early years—because he was ADOPTED. The word that had previously been worn as a medal around his neck, an honor to have been chosen, became unkind and undesirable. He had been an unwanted, abandoned child. The rejection he felt took root and would burden him into adulthood.

Children do not often have the capability of understanding how their words and actions can cause pain and rejection in the hearts of others. At six years old, Randy did not have the capability or the words to express his feelings of rejection and the burden he felt, so he did the only thing he knew to do: fight. As a result of the name-calling and the hurt that became lodged deep in Randy's heart, Randy became an unruly and outraged student. He fought for his place among his peers, his place at home, and his place among his church friends to prove to himself and others that he was valuable and worth being a part of their lives.

At school, he spent such an immense amount of time in trouble that the teacher moved his desk next to hers. Somehow that teacher conveyed to Randy that he was so important to her that she wanted him right next to her. He could not wait to tell his parents that she liked him so much that she moved his desk all the way to the front of the room, next to hers—and he was now her assistant! Moving his desk was the only way she could direct his anger and frustration into positive channels and keep him from being disruptive. As he grew up, he understood that he was NOT the teacher's pet but her special project. What a fantastic teacher!

||||||||||||||||||||||||||||||||||||||||||||||||||||||||||||||||||||||||||||||||||||||

Randy could not wait to tell his
parents that his teacher liked
him so much that she moved
his desk all the way to the front
of the room, next to hers—and
he was now her assistant!

According to the Association for Psychological Science, research suggests that, while babies are in the womb, they can feel the emotions of their birth mother.[4] Randy's birth mother relayed her rejection and anger to him before he was ever born. The anger and

---

4   Association for Psychological Science, "Can fetus sense mother's psychological state? Study suggests yes," ScienceDaily, 10 November 2011. <www.sciencedaily.com/releases/2011/11/111110142352.htm>.

rejection that had taken root in Randy's heart went deeper and became more painful in the subsequent years, feeding on itself and making Randy believe that no one loved him, no one could ever love him, and he was entirely unlovable. Although feelings are not fact, the feelings became real to Randy. He believed the lie.

Isn't this just like the enemy of our souls? He whispers untruths into our spirits, and we begin to believe what he says. Satan's lie becomes truth to us, and, although there is no basis for that "truth," it becomes a part of who we are. Randy's family loved him immensely, but after he began to believe Satan's lie, no amount of reinforcement of their love could convince him. How could they love someone who was not really their son, who was not of their blood? It was only when Randy reached the age of twelve, through another miracle, that he began to understand how a person could genuinely love someone who was not a true blood relation.

Life was hard and bitterly cold in upstate New York. The family lived in a small, drafty house on Rock Street. There was no bathroom in the house, making an outhouse necessary for relieving themselves. Using the outhouse in the summertime was not nearly as bad as using it in the winter. Ever the entrepreneur, Randy could recall charging the neighborhood boys a quarter to come in and see their "outside bathroom." No one else in the neighborhood had one like theirs. I can imagine some of the comments and conversations that occurred among those little boys who paid to see the hole (and the stuff inside the hole) in the outside bathroom. Randy generated quite a bit of revenue until his mom found out and immediately stopped it. She even made him return the money.

In the winter, ice would form on the house's inside windows. The boys could see their breath in the air when they got out of bed in the mornings. It seemed that no matter how much wood they put into the fireplace, the house would never get warm enough to heat the rooms upstairs.

Both Randy's father, Norman, and his grandfather, Raymond, worked at Endicott Forge, a steel fabricating plant where the company kept wages as low as possible. There was very little opportunity to increase the family income, and employee strikes were common. Norman took on additional jobs to help with the family income, working before and after his hours at the steel plant. Even with the extra hours, work, and wages, there was not nearly enough money to meet the needs of growing boys, and there was too much month left at the end of the money.

After much deliberation, Norman and June decided that the best way to increase their standard of living would be for Norman to go back into the military and make a career in the US Navy. They did not know where this career change would take them, only that it was their best opportunity for advancement in life. Little did they know that they were placing another thread in the tapestry that would continue the work that God was weaving for Randy's life.

LIFE IN TEXAS

After leaving New York, the family moved to Texas for a short time. Here, Randy and Jeff envisioned themselves as cowboys, dressing appropriately, spending time in the desert, and camping. On one family camping trip, Randy had an up-close and personal encounter with an armadillo. He was sure this unusual creature was going to attack and kill him. Randy, ever the cowboy, had his trusty BB gun with him and began to shoot at the armadillo—of course, never phasing the prehistoric creature who wore a coat of armor! Randy backed away and continued to shoot as the animal approached him. Unfortunately, Randy backed himself right over a cactus, and he spent the remainder of the camping trip with his mom and aunts removing cactus spines from his backside.

LIFE IN VIRGINIA

As time went on and life unfolded for Randy, the family found itself moving again and living in Virginia, embracing the military life. Randy's early life of anger and frustration had followed him to Texas, and they now became evident in Virginia. To help temper his aggression, Randy began to play sports, football being one of his favorites. This helped him channel his energy more productively and not get into so much trouble at school. In Randy's words, football made it okay for him to hit something hard and fast with no repercussions.

Randy was twelve years old, and Jeff was eleven when June became unexpectedly pregnant with another son. This pregnancy was difficult and wrought with problems. When the baby was prematurely delivered, the doctors found that June had uterine cancer. It was a miracle that the tiny baby had survived the pregnancy and was born with no congenital disabilities or abnormalities.

At that time, June was working as a personal assistant at the Christian Broadcasting Network, and people throughout the network began to pray, asking God for a miracle. She underwent an emergency hysterectomy, and for many days thereafter, her survival was not ensured. Although the atmosphere was tense and unsure, Randy was allowed to hold his new, tiny baby brother, Raymond, in his arms. At that time, Randy fell in love with his little brother and immediately understood how a person could love someone that was not related to them by blood. Raymond was his little brother, and Randy loved him completely. God performed a miracle of love at that moment, giving Randy a little glimpse of what it meant to love and be loved—with no expectations or prerequisites. A bond of love, not of blood, was forged that continued for their entire lives.

||||||||||||||||||||||||||||||||||||||||||||||||||||||||||||||||||||||||||||||||||||||

> When Randy held Raymond in his arms, he fell in love with his baby brother and immediately understood how a person could love someone that was not related to them by blood.

While June was hanging between life and death, Randy began to overhear conversations between his aunts and uncles. They were trying to decide where the boys would live if June did not recover, who would raise the baby, and what Norman would do without June around to take care of the family. After one such conversation, Randy remonstrated his family and declared that his mother would live and not die and that the family would be whole. He was only twelve years old but had already determined that the Word of God was true. June had read the Word of God to Randy and Jeff every day of their lives, giving them a foundation of strong faith. Randy now felt the responsibility to see that his extended family also believed. Randy later told me that this was the first time he remembered supernatural boldness being displayed in his life.

June recovered from her surgery, and further treatment was unnecessary. Baby Raymond began to grow and thrive, and the family eventually relocated to Goose Creek, South Carolina, continuing their military lives. In Goose Creek, Randy discovered that having a baby brother in tow most of the time was also beneficial in impressing the female population. Randy told me that he made sure he had his chick magnet (Baby Raymond) with him before he went anywhere that he knew girls would be. Randy's time with Raymond also helped prepare him for becoming a father to our daughters many years later. He had no learning curve in changing diapers, feeding, burping, or clothing babies.

LIFE IN SOUTH CAROLINA

Randy began to sense even more that the destiny of God was on his life in Goose Creek. The family became involved in a local church, Northwoods Assembly, and Randy had a true encounter with a God who loves and understands the deepest pain in our hearts. Although Randy's parents had always told him that God had His hand upon his life, Randy still struggled with rejection and a sense of not belonging. There was anger in his heart that he fought against daily. However, it was also at this time that Randy decided the family he had was enough for him, and he didn't need to know any more about his birth parents. In his mind, his birth parents were either too poor to keep him or were having an affair. He was partially right on both accounts. In his mind, he did not need to know anymore.

By the time he reached age fifteen, Randy felt that God had called him into ministry during a youth camp. Due to his insecurities, Randy stuttered and was afraid to speak in front of people. When he was required to speak in front of the class, he would take a failing grade rather than do so. Whenever he stood before people, his voice would shake, and he had to breathe deeply to force himself to relax. He did not know how he would ever preach or teach, but he was willing to attempt whatever God asked him to do: public speaking, teaching, or mentoring.

||||||||||||||||||||||||||||||||||||||||||||||||||||||||||||||||||||||||||||||||||||

> He did not know how he would ever preach or teach, but he was willing to attempt whatever God asked him to do: public speaking, teaching, or mentoring.

After returning from the youth camp, Randy told his pastor, and the pastor then told the church that Randy had answered the call of God to be a minister. After the service that night, one of the girls in the youth group approached Randy and told him that she thought God could use anyone but him! Randy agreed with her. She knew Randy's life, but she didn't know our God.

Randy continued to play football in high school and found that he could also share the gospel of Jesus Christ with his teammates both on and off the field. Randy found his first mission field to be his teammates and high school friends. He discovered the joy of winning others to Christ, and at one time, the entire football team was attending church with him. The team became a force to be reckoned with in the youth group at Northwoods Assembly and school. A revival of paramount proportions began to happen among his peers, changing the hearts and lives of athletes, academics, and artists in Goose Creek High School.

Miles, one of Randy's close friends and a football player on his team, gave his heart to Christ, and Miles became a frequent fixture in the Valimont home. Throughout the remainder of their high school careers, Miles and Randy were almost inseparable. This was during a time when racial tensions were extremely high, and as they were of different races, their friendship was out of the norm.

White people and African Americans did not normally become close friends, but Randy and Miles proved that it could be done. Neither saw the color of their skin. They only heard the cry of their hearts to be loved and accepted by one another. Their friendship set the tone for acceptance, and they became leaders in their school to help alleviate racial tension. Randy's friendship with Miles also helped Randy understand part of the African American culture and strengthened his desire to see fully integrated churches under his leadership.

When Randy submitted to the call of God on his life, June was overjoyed. Although she had been unable to fulfill the call of God on her life to go into missions, God was going to use one of her sons in her place. She had made and fulfilled her promise to God, and God had answered her prayer. Randy truly belonged to God, and God was going to use him—far beyond anything she or anyone could imagine.

Whether weaving a tapestry or putting together a puzzle, you will never understand or envision the end result unless you are looking at a representation of how the masterpiece will appear when it is finished. When God is weaving the tapestry of our lives, we often have no idea what He is doing with us, and we cannot see the pattern or the finished picture when we are living it! It is only as the tapestry continues to be woven that we see the beautiful emerging image.

||||||||||||||||||||||||||||||||||||||||||||||||||||||||||||||||||||||||||||||||||||||||

When God is weaving the tapestry of our lives, we often have no idea what He is doing with us, and we cannot see the pattern or the finished picture when we are living it!

CHAPTER 4

THE WEAVING CONTINUES

LAKELAND, FLORIDA: COLLEGE

In planning to fulfill his life's goals, Randy became somewhat distracted and decided to be a businessman and a preacher. He desired to do both, and ever the overachiever, he thought he could! He graduated early from high school, at age sixteen, turning down a scholarship to Clemson University to attend a local college and earn a business degree. As he attended the local college that first semester, he realized he had made a mistake and needed to attend Bible college full time.

He recognized that he felt a deep desire to study the things of God and a dissatisfaction in his current course of study. One of his mentors had told him that if he felt he could do anything other than ministry, he needed to do it. However, if he could do nothing else with his life other than ministry, he must have been, indeed, called by God! Randy finished his current semester at the local college and then made plans to pursue a degree in pastoral leadership/theology. He finally understood that his call to ministry was all-or-nothing. He would do nothing without giving it 100 percent of his time and effort.

Randy continued to follow God's plan for his life and, in doing so, decided to attend Southeastern College (now University) to prepare for full-time ministry. Once he made the decision, Randy had to determine how he would pay for his education. It was one thing to attend a local college, live at home, and work when he didn't have classes, but it would be quite a step of faith to go away to school without the proper funds.

Attending Southeastern College was an expensive and faith-building endeavor. A student could live on-campus, eat in the cafeteria, purchase books, and attend classes while putting all the expenses on their school bill. Grants and loans often did not arrive for students until the semester was well underway. Only then could the money be applied to the school bill. The problem that students often faced was that one could attend the entire semester, putting expenses on their school bill, but they could not take final exams until the entire bill was paid.

Randy attended that first semester but had no money to pay his school bill. He had made his decision to attend after the deadline for applying for financial aid, so no money was forthcoming. On the final night before exams, Randy walked around the campus praying and wondering if he had missed God's plan. He did not know what he would do the next day without money to pay his bill. Should he pack? Leave? Call his parents again to see if there was a little bit they could send? Beg the administration to allow him to take his exams? God assured Randy that He would meet the need, but Randy had no evidence of that. He later told me that as he walked the campus and the lakeside around the campus, he was reminded of these scriptures and began to recite them repeatedly to himself:

"For as the body without the spirit is dead,
so faith without works is dead also."
—James 2:26 (KJV)

"Now faith is the substance of things hoped
for, the evidence of things not seen."
—Hebrews 11:1 (KJV)

As Randy walked, he began to learn to operate in faith and exercise what he knew God was doing in his life. He had to learn to live by faith and trust that God would do what He said.

||||||||||||||||||||||||||||||||||||||||||||||||||||||||||||||||||||||||||||||||||||||||||||||||||

His act of faith in attending Bible college and following the call of God on his life was confirmed by his uncle's gift. It was all the evidence he needed.

Randy spent a tumultuous night, not knowing his next steps. He was disheartened as he walked to his mailbox on the way to the financial aid office the next morning to withdraw from school. In the mailbox, Randy found a letter from an uncle who lived quite a distance away. In the letter was a check for the entire amount he needed to pay his school bill, tithe on the money that was sent, and have enough left over to go to Steak and Shake for a hamburger! There was no need to withdraw, and he could take the final exams that semester. His act of faith in attending Bible college and following the call of God on his life was confirmed by his uncle's gift. It was all the evidence he needed. He knew he was on the right path to fulfilling the destiny of God.

He finished the semester and returned to his home, unsure if his next step would be another semester of college or stepping into full-time ministry. Although God had provided the funds and met every need for that first semester, Randy struggled with the idea of returning to college. In his mind, a college degree was unnecessary and expensive, and how valuable could it be? Couldn't he learn from his pastor, listen to other ministers, study on his own, and be just as effective? As he dug ditches that summer, God spoke to his heart, and Randy decided that his next step would be to return to college and finish what he had started.

Finishing became a constant theme in our lives. Randy often spoke of a conversation he had with his father about quitting. Norman told him that it would really bother him the first time he quit a task, a sport, or a job. The next time, it would bother him but not quite as much. Then, if he continued quitting, he would come to a place where it would not bother him at all. It would become a viable option and easy to do! Finishing what we started became one of our family values, and I do not remember that we, as a couple or as a family, walked away from a job undone when we had the choice.

Within a few short days of our return to college, Randy's and my paths intersected again. Randy was now the roommate of a good friend of mine. The three of us began to spend more and more time together, both Randy and I swearing off dating relationships for a time. My friend, Bubba, decided not to continue that semester but to return to his home in Tennessee. Since Randy and I were already spending time together, we continued. It was almost as if we had become a friendship habit.

Neither of us knew that God had not only placed those dreams in our hearts, but He was weaving them deep within us so that we would, one day, use those dreams to fulfill part of His plan for us.

We met both by accident and by design during lunches and dinners. We sometimes sat together in chapel services and had many heart-to-heart conversations about God's plan for our lives and what we envisioned our future would be. Randy told me that he desired to one day be the pastor of a large church, not for the numbers but for the ability to influence and equip others to share the gospel! When I told him that I believed he would, he was startled that someone else could believe in his dream. I, in turn, expressed to him my desire to teach in a public-school setting and possibly use my teaching skills in overseas mission projects. Neither of us knew that God had not only placed those dreams in our hearts, but He was weaving them deep within us so that we would, one day, use those dreams to fulfill part of His plan for us.

It was during those quiet conversations in the chapel and in the quiet places that Randy told me he was adopted, never knew his birth family, and had no desire to do so. He told me that he was Italian and that many of his close friends were Italian, so I did not question his information. During that time, Randy became a spiritual leader in my life, encouraging me to submit to what God was calling me to be.

One night, we were with a large group of our friends at a local library when I began to pour out my heart to Randy, telling him about my ministry hurts as a pastor's daughter. I expressed my determination NEVER to be a pastor's wife. Randy looked at me with compassion in his eyes and emphatically said, "Jelly, you will be a pastor's wife. That is your destiny." I looked into his eyes and realized that God was speaking through him into my heart and that maybe, just maybe, he was correct. Maybe God did want me to be in ministry, and maybe I needed to let go of the ministry hurts I had already experienced.

As Randy spoke those words to me, he later told me that the Holy Spirit quietly spoke into his spirit, saying, *She will be a minister's wife, and she will be yours.* Thank God that Randy did not say that part to me until much later! I had avoided ministry men all my dating years, and I would have run as fast as my short legs would carry me. All a young man had to do to end a relationship with me was to tell me that he felt a call of God on his life to be a minister. Somehow, without me realizing it, my friendship with Randy would blossom into something more, and it would not matter to me if Randy, now my best friend, did go into ministry if we were in it together.

Randy and I were both from lower-middle-class families and had little to no expendable income while we were dating. Many of our dates consisted of time spent in the library (which helped raise our GPAs), walking around campus late at night (trying to keep the required six inches of distance between us!), and walking around the many lakes in Lakeland. We were chased by ducks and geese around Lake Morton, stung by fire ants around Lake Spence, and eaten by mosquitos around Lake Mirror. We dreamed of life after college around Lake Hollingsworth.

It was during those times of quiet conversation, relaxation, and play that I began to see cracks in Randy's strong confidence. In these relaxed times, he expressed his need to be accepted and loved for who he was. He often spoke of the mysterious birth family who gave him away and why anyone would do that to an infant. I also discovered that Randy was one of the most loyal and forgiving people that I would ever meet. If anyone did something wrong to him, he would quickly forgive them. He had a very quick temper but was also quick to let offenses go. When it was over, it was truly over. Often the anger Randy had was based on his perceived rejection of himself by others.

As Randy slowly revealed his personality to me and I revealed mine to him, we found that we both had the potential to be quite opinionated. Strong-willed, stubborn, or bullheaded (a Tennessee term), we both had the potential to dig our heels into the ground to fight for what was important to us. That would be one of the most critical aspects of our relationship and our ministry as we anticipated what God would do in our future life together.

We spent many hours together as a couple and nurtured our relationships with our other friends. We had seen many couples begin dating and essentially throw away their friendships to spend time together as a couple exclusively. We determined that, although we enjoyed being together, we also needed to nurture friendships outside of our own. Randy was an expert at having lots of good friends and taking time to hear the hearts of those around him. It is one of the things that made him such a great leader. He carried many of those relationships through the end of his life.

It was during our sophomore year of college, just after we began dating, that God heard Randy's prayers to be used. Randy was invited by Pastor Frank Severance to become his weekend youth pastor at a church in Oxford, Florida. Randy continued his studies during the week, but the time spent in his weekend ministry allowed him to be productive, put his knowledge to work, begin developing sermons, and have a little spending money for that next week. Randy would often return from his weekend in Oxford, seek me out, and tell me of all the great things God had done that weekend among his students. It wasn't long before he invited me to go to Oxford with him to minister in music at the church. We spent the weekends with Pastor Severance and his family, enjoying their Italian lifestyle, which was a phenomenal respite from college life.

On Sunday evenings, after the service, the pastor's wife or daughter would hand us a bag of bologna sandwiches, chips, and drinks for our return trip to Lakeland. I think they were the best sandwiches I ever had in my life, maybe because we were so tired, so hungry, and so depleted of our energy. Our time together as we traveled to and from Oxford was precious as we continued to share our hopes and dreams. I think I became one of Randy's "projects" as he would always ask me as we drove away from the pastor's home, "What did God speak to you this weekend, Jelly?" There was always an answer for him, even if it was, "I am too tired to even articulate it now, Randy!"

Both Randy and I were on the Student Government Association. He represented the sophomore class, and I represented my dormitory. Our weekly meetings were on Monday nights and were always very important to attend. One Monday night, I was particularly troubled by the direction our relationship was taking, and I told Randy I needed to talk to him. It must have been inevitable as we spent so much time together, both during the week and on weekends, that my feelings would grow. I needed to know if we were headed into a long-term relationship or a dear friendship. We had about an hour before our meeting, so we hopped into his red Vega and headed to beautiful Lake Mirror in downtown Lakeland to have a chat.

During that quiet time together, I expressed to Randy that I was beginning to have deeper feelings for him than that of a friend. I told him that if I was not someone with whom he could fall in love, take home to his mother, and spend the rest of his life that I didn't want to spend so much exclusive time together. I would not be part of his youth ministry and travel with him, and I would not provide the music for the church services in Oxford. I was not in love with him, but I knew my emotions were headed that way. I needed to protect myself from a future heartbreak if there was the possibility of one. Randy was very quiet and did not respond. I had no expectations about how the conversation would unfold, but I certainly did not expect him to say nothing.

Randy and I got into his car and headed back to the student government meeting. He disappeared afterward and avoided me for the next three weeks. He later told me that I had scared him. He knew what God had told him outside the library at Florida

Southern, and I had unintentionally confirmed it. I continued with my social life, acting as if I were fine and thanking God that I had avoided a heartbreak, as it appeared Randy was a "player!" Confirming Randy's idea that I was flirtatious, I dated—lots—and spent more time with friends and focusing on my studies.

One day, Randy came to my dorm to continue the conversation that had begun three weeks previously. He told me that he did not know where our relationship was going, but he did miss our time together and wanted to continue our close friendship. I agreed to resume our close friendship, and we again started to spend time together, putting our other dating relationships aside.

> As often happens in close friendships, the more time we spent together, the more time we wanted to be together, and we fell deeply in love before completing that semester.

As often happens in close friendships, the more time we spent together, the more time we wanted to be together, and we fell deeply in love before completing that semester. I had settled in my heart that God was calling me into ministry, just as He had called Randy, and we would spend our lives following God's plan, side by side. We were engaged the following summer and married at the end of our junior year of college, finishing our undergraduate degrees as a married couple.

Just before my father walked me down the aisle, we stopped, and he had a father-daughter conversation with me. He looked me in the eyes and said, "I just want you to know that if you have any doubts, or you don't want to do this, you can walk away right now!"

I was startled and quickly replied, "No, I want to do this."

My father continued, "All right, but you need to know that as you walk down the aisle to marry Randy, you are not just walking toward a man, but you are walking into ministry. This is forever, and you will no longer have the option to walk away. Should you choose to walk away, you will answer to God, not to man."

I nervously put one foot in front of the other and walked toward Randy, into marriage, and into ministry. We both understood that God was calling us as a couple to do something supernatural. Part of my wedding vows to Randy were taken from the book of Ruth as she stated to her dearly loved mother-in-law,

> *"Wherever you go, I will go; And wherever you lodge, I will lodge; Your people shall be my people, and your God my God."*
> —Ruth 1:16, NKJV

That became a vow of my heart to Randy's as we walked out our marriage of almost forty years.

MARRIAGE AND MINISTRY, 101

The first year of marriage was challenging. I had no idea of what to expect in a marriage, and neither did he, but we knew we were totally committed. Randy was from a family of three boys, two parents, a military lifestyle, and weekends on the beach. I was from a family of three girls, two parents, a ministry lifestyle, and week-ends at church. Putting those two opposing lifestyles, hormonal reactions, and expectations together, along with both of us working and going to school full-time proved challenging at best.

One of the things that helped strengthen our relationship is that we were so far away from both sets of parents. Randy's family was four hundred miles away, and mine was eight hundred miles away. If we had a problem, we had no one else to call or discuss our issues. Telephone calls were expensive, and there was no social media! As a result, we learned to work through our problems—sometimes quickly and sometimes not so quickly. Another thing that I think helped us immensely was our determination not to quit. We learned to compromise with one another, and divorce was never an option, never a word that we threw around in moments of anger and frustration. We learned the fundamental lesson to leave our families and cleave to one another.

|||||||||||||||||||||||||||||||||||||||||||||||||||||||||||||||||||||||||||||||||||||||

We learned the fundamental
lesson to leave our families
and cleave to one another.

One of the things that became a significant part of our marriage preparation was a visit to my physician. Due to female issues, my doctor told me that I would probably never be able to conceive a child. When Randy and I discussed this, Randy emphatically told me that we would not accept the doctor's report, but we would believe the report of the Lord and be fruitful and multiply. I returned to the doctor, who told me that some things seemed to be corrected. Although I might conceive, I would possibly be on bed rest the entire pregnancy and probably have a Cesarean delivery. Again, Randy told me that we would believe the report of the Lord and be fruitful and multiply. Randy's faith was much stronger than mine, but I tried to trust along with him.

We completed our final year of college in April 1981, one month before celebrating our first anniversary. We spent one week vacationing and a second week packing. We then traveled to Springdale, Arkansas, where we began our first full-time position as youth pastors. Randy and I thrived there and loved what God had called us to do.

Randy developed relationships with our students that continued throughout their lives. He planned and facilitated events that no one else had ever done. He visited schools and spoke to students about life choices, and he told his story of rejection. He coached football, so he could spend time with students in athletics. He taught school as a substitute, so he could have one-on-one time with students. After a particular day of teaching, he realized that he probably was not in his best element as he held a disrespectful, aggressive student against the wall by his shirt. He never accepted another substitute teaching position after that.

Unfortunately, I could not get a teaching job during our first school year in Arkansas, so I did whatever I could find to do and get a paycheck. One of the first jobs I had was working for a company that cleaned up for insurance companies after fires or other disasters. I often came home from work covered in soot and grime from head to toe, tracking the mess I brought from work into our apartment. When I arrived home from work, Randy would look at me and ask me to shower before doing anything else. We probably spent more money on soap, water, and shampoo than I made while working for the disaster company.

We spent weekends doing youth activities, going to high school and college football games, playing handball, ice skating, planning fifth quarter events, having students in our home, and arranging any other happenings Randy could envision. Still, we were happy to be married and working together in ministry.

The youth group, which we named "New Wine," immediately began to grow. Randy's passion for God, his limitless dreams, students from the University of Arkansas, and a local Youth With a Mission (YWAM) group all caused the group to expand. One of the young ladies who attended our youth group was a budding music artist from the area. One night, she came into our service and debuted a song she had just written. Twyla told us that her dad was not a big fan of her latest song, but she wanted to sing it for us anyway. Twyla Paris later recorded and released her song, "The Warrior is a Child," which became one of her greatest hits. We always felt honored that she sang it for our youth group first.

God was moving in our hearts, giving Randy the confidence that he needed to achieve what God called him to do. The ministry was growing, and many of our students began to feel that God was also calling them into ministry. Throughout our lives, we stayed connected and enjoyed many of the relationships that began at First Assembly of God in Springdale, Arkansas. Randy knew that he was fulfilling God's purpose and the destiny of God in his life and that for some reason, maybe for our students, God had given him life.

After living in Arkansas for one year, I received a contract for a teaching job in Pea Ridge, a small town north of us in the mountains. Most of my students were children from migrant families who worked in the local poultry houses. I was so excited to teach and train these students. One of the first lessons I had to teach was the importance of cleaning their shoes before they walked into the classroom.

It seemed that the children in each family had a job to do before coming to school. According to one student, Brett, they had to get up the turkeys "piled" in the night. I had no perspective until he explained to me that sometimes turkeys would fall down on top of one another and die in the night. (I didn't know turkeys were not smart enough to get up!) Brett had to pick up the dead turkeys and burn them before coming to school. I had to give a little instruction to Brett and the other students that whatever they took from the turkey house on their shoes could not come into my classroom.

My first week of teaching was eventful as I came home to tell Randy I sent twenty of my forty students home with head lice that day. He knew I was extremely traumatized by finding so many students with these little parasites. As we lay in bed that night, Randy looked at me with mischievousness and quietly asked me not to cuddle with him but to move my head to my own pillow as he wasn't sure if I also had head lice. The concern was legitimate! After he picked the feathers from the pillow out of his teeth, he changed his mind about our cuddle time. Every day, there was another story of third-grade students from me or middle and high school students from him to share with one another. Some of the stories were filled with heartache, but others were filled with laughter. We learned to laugh at ourselves and others as we lived our dreams. Life was fun as our love for one another deepened and matured, and God continued to weave our tapestry—our lives—together.

||||||||||||||||||||||||||||||||||||||||||||||||||||||||||||||||||||||||||||||||||||||

We learned to laugh at ourselves and others as we lived our dreams.

During my second year of teaching, three years into our marriage, and contrary to my doctor's diagnosis, God gave us a daughter whom we named Jordan. She was the first grandchild on both sides of our family and became the reigning princess in our lives. I had no issues becoming pregnant, no problems during the pregnancy, and taught school until two days before she was born. Both the labor and delivery were quick, only seven hours, with no complications.

For the first time in his life, Randy held in his arms someone who was a blood relative. Jordan was beautiful and perfect, and we both fell deeply in love with her, doting on her as most first-time parents dote on their children! We were no exception!

During one of our many conversations about what to expect with our new baby, Randy warned me that since he didn't know his genetics, there was no way to anticipate how our new baby would look—light or dark skin, eye color, hair color and texture, etc. Of course, that did not matter to either of us as all we desired was a healthy baby. When she was born, both Randy and his parents thought Jordan looked just like him. She had a head full of dark curls, thus explaining my incessant heartburn (according to old wives' tales), and the most beautiful olive skin. We both wondered where the skin tone came from but knew that Randy tended to get very tanned in the summer sun. It was not a big issue. We didn't know that Jordan was genetically predisposed to olive skin and dark curly hair.

Due to the incredible growth in our youth ministry, many pastors throughout the nation began to call Randy and ask him to consider making a move to one of their churches. We weren't sure what we needed to do, but we began to consider many options. We knew our position would soon change as our current pastor, my father, was preparing to relocate to Gainesville, Georgia. One winter day, shortly after Jordan's birth, Randy and I traveled to Tulsa, Oklahoma, to speak with a pastor about the possibility of moving and becoming part of his church staff. Randy was sure this was to be our next ministry position! I cried as we returned home, unsure of this next step and if it were in the plan of God, the tapestry that God was weaving for us. Randy was sure that my emotional state was due to post-pregnancy hormones, but I was not quite as sure.

Randy was quite angry and didn't understand why I could not "feel good" about this next step. He interpreted my misgivings as rejection. He took me home, admittedly frustrated with me, and decided he would go to the church to pray. Just before he left our home, he said to me, "I am the head of this house, and I will make the decision based on what I think is best for this family. You told me in our wedding vows that wherever I went you would go, that you would live where I lived, and your people would be my people, and my God would be your God!"

Oh, yes, I did, but it was SO not a good thing to say to a post-pregnancy female. I didn't know that, although God had begun preparing my heart for change, he was also preparing both Randy and me to learn to hear his voice. It seemed as if at that time in our lives, God chose to use moments of supernatural leading, moments of epiphany to direct us in our next steps. We relied on God's supernatural leading many times over the next thirty-five years.

While Randy was at the church complaining to God about his stubborn wife and genuinely seeking the plan of God for both of us, the Lord directed him to this scripture:

So they got up early in the morning and went out into the **Wilderness of Tekoa***; and as they went out, Jehoshaphat stood and said, "Hear me, O Judah, and you inhabitants of Jerusalem! Believe and trust in the Lord your God and you will be established (secure). Believe and trust in His prophets and succeed.*
—2 Chronicles 20:20 (author paraphrase and emphasis)

What an odd scripture to which God would direct him. However, just before Randy headed home, he received a call. It was from the assistant district superintendent of Georgia, Dr. L. M. Addison, asking him if he would be interested in coming to Georgia to pastor a church in "Toccoa. . . ." Spelled differently, pronounced the same. A moment of epiphany.

We traveled to Toccoa shortly after that. As we drove over the Georgia mountains between Gainesville and Toccoa, Randy marveled at what a wilderness it seemed to be, with few homes and no businesses, mostly forests and dense foliage. The church we visited was small and had a history of problems. As the service began, Randy kept waiting for people to arrive, assuming that they were just late. It took him a moment to realize that all the people had already arrived. As I remember, about thirty-five people attended that day—including children and babies.

This church was smaller than our youth group of almost one hundred students, and Randy searched his heart to try to understand why God was mad at him and why God would make him start over. Randy did not understand at that time that God had so much more to teach us, and we needed to be in a safe place for Him to do so. Glad Tidings in Toccoa provided that place. We were young enough that the church people would excuse our youthful mistakes and wise enough to own the mistakes we made and not try to excuse them.

||||||||||||||||||||||||||||||||||||||||||||||||||||||||||||||||||||||||||||||||

We were young enough that the church people would excuse our youthful mistakes and wise enough to own the mistakes we made and not try to excuse them.

Randy preached that morning to the best of his ability, and I sang the special music. After the service, two people came to the altar and gave their hearts to Christ. I didn't know it at the time, but Randy had prayed and asked the Lord that if this move was in His divine plan that someone would make a commitment to the Lord during the services that day. When so few people came to the morning service, Randy was sure that God would not answer. God proved him wrong, and it was another indication that we were moving to Toccoa.

That night, Randy and I left Toccoa and headed back to Arkansas, driving the entire night as I had to be back at school the following day to teach my class. As we drove, the church members had a business meeting and voted 99 percent for us to become their new pastors. The one dissenting vote was from the church organist, who felt Randy just might be too young to be a pastor. When they told Randy about her concern, he expressed to the church board that she was correct. He was too young to be a pastor. The board member told Mrs. Louise that Randy agreed with her, and when he did, she changed her vote. That meant that we were voted in at 100 percent. How rare it is that a church congregation can agree to that extent! Although we understood that this type of move would be difficult, a unanimous vote like this increased Randy's confidence in who he was and what God called him to do. It also added a little balm to soothe some of the deep pain of rejection in his heart.

TOCCOA, GEORGIA

Within a few days of returning to our home in Arkansas, we agreed to take the position of senior/lead/only pastor at Glad Tidings Assembly of God in Toccoa, Georgia. We knew we would take a $20,000 pay cut and would need to live on our savings and the food in our freezer—at least for a few months. We packed up our family and moved with our little four-month-old daughter, arriving for our first Sunday on April Fool's Day 1984. Randy joked at how ironic it was that this day would be our first Sunday and hoped it did not set a precedent for the coming years.

Just before we left Arkansas, one of our friends in the church gave us a cow. All we had to do was pay to have it slaughtered and processed. It was available just before we moved. The meat from this blessing became our only source of protein during our first year in Toccoa, but we ate well. I also discovered in this time that Randy had more generosity in him than I had ever envisioned. One day he came home and told me to get a bag of beef ready to give away. I was shocked as I knew we could not afford to replace it once it was gone. I asked him how much he wanted, and he said at least ten pounds. I opened the freezer and counted out some of our steaks, roasts, and ground beef. I placed it in a bag, and out the door he went! He returned home about twenty minutes later, having given away what I had packed for him.

The following Sunday, a man walked up to me and told me that God had supernaturally blessed his family that week. They had two teenage sons, no groceries, and no money to buy any food. They didn't know what they were going to do. They were looking around their house trying to find coins to buy some milk and heard a knock at the door. Thinking it was probably a bill collector, they ignored the knock for a few minutes. When they looked on the front porch, no one was there. But a bag of various cuts of beef was sitting on the steps. They had no idea where it came from, but it met the need for that week. Of course, I did not tell them that Randy was the food delivery person that day. Throughout our lives, I repeatedly witnessed Randy's generosity. We did not know, but we would eventually discover that his paternal birth family was also reputed to be extremely generous people.

We struggled through those first few months in Toccoa. I accepted the job of administrating the Little Learners Christian Learning Center at the church, in addition to being the worship leader for our small church and a new mom. Randy worked hard. He visited over one hundred people each week, ministering to the sick and the weary. He invited people to church, sought ways for us to cut personal expenses, brought home gifts of food from parishioners, and budgeted to help us keep our heads above water financially. I never knew how he had the energy or the drive to do all he did, but in retrospect, I believe he needed to prove to himself that he could accomplish what God had called him to do.

One of the gifts that God gave to us during those first few years in Toccoa was retired pastor George Samuelson and his precious sister, Edith. Brother Samuelson showed Randy the town, the businessmen, the slums, the projects, and Toccoa Falls Bible College. In essence, George Samuelson showed Randy the ropes of Toccoa. He was a small Swede, lived next door to the church, and since he was retired, spent a lot of time in the church offices and doing little jobs around the church.

One day, Brother Samuelson walked into Randy's office soaking wet with an odd request. He couldn't get the baptistry emptied. The night before, we'd had a baptism service, and the chain to empty the baptistry fell into the water. He could not reach it and needed Randy to push him down into the water and hold him down until he could retrieve the chain, pull out the stopper, and empty the baptistry! Randy was appalled. He suggested that Brother Samuelson wait until Randy could get to the job and do it, but Brother Samuelson was adamant that it needed to be done immediately. Randy told me that he could only envision the newspaper headlines the following day stating, "Boy Preacher Drowns Elderly Minister in Local Church Baptistry." When Randy refused to hold him under, Brother Samuelson called him a wimp and went back to his task. After multiple tries, he was finally able to retrieve the plug without Randy's help!

Time went on, God began to move in the church services, and the church began to grow. We had many commitments for salvation, and many were baptized in the Holy Spirit. With the help of devoted parishioners, we organized the choir, the worship, and the media ministry—three microphones, a monitor, a sound board, and an overhead projector. We helped revamp the girls' and boys' clubs, the nursery, food ministry, and any other ministry we could envision. We were content knowing that this was all a part of God's overall plan. There was so much we were learning about people and ministry. Although I had been raised in a pastor's home and knew a bit about ministry, being a pastor's wife put a completely different spin on my knowledge and experience.

||||||||||||||||||||||||||||||||||||||||||||||||||||||||||||||||||||||||||||||||

> When Randy refused to
> hold him under, Brother
> Samuelson called him a wimp
> and went back to his task.

During those first few weeks in Toccoa, Randy found that the church was desperately behind in finances. They were in arrears to the bank, the national Assemblies of God loan department, local utility companies, local businesses, and the former pastor. This was one of the reasons they were so anxious to find a pastor to lead them, regardless of his age! After being given the information, Randy felt as if he had somehow failed us, his family. He didn't get all the information before accepting the position. There was no way he could handle the kind of debt this church had incurred. All his insecurities came rushing back, along with the voice of the enemy telling him that he was not good enough. Who did he think he was trying to lead a group of people like this? What did he have to say that others would listen to?

But. God. How I love those two little words! Satan tried to destroy what God had begun, but God had a plan much bigger than Satan ever thought. God began to teach Randy how to handle the debt and what to do to help the church grow. Randy began to call and visit the businesses to which the church owed money. He made commitments to them that the church would pay their bill and that we would do our best to see it paid quickly. Every week, the church applied a little bit of money to each debt. As church finances grew, the debt was slowly whittled away.

||||||||||||||||||||||||||||||||||||||||||||||||||||||||||||||||||||||||||||||||||

But. God. How I love those two little words!

We were just getting settled into our new town when a member of the local Civil Air Patrol stopped by the office to chat with Randy about our church daycare. It seemed that in addition to church financial problems, the daycare was in big, big trouble. One of the teachers was selling drugs out of the center during the children's nap time, and people in the community knew it. At that time, officials planned to raid the daycare in the coming days. I am not sure if this gentleman was breaking protocol or if someone instructed him to contact Randy, but he did. Never a person to shy away from confrontation, Randy immediately went to the daycare, asked the appropriate questions, and fired the responsible woman. Law enforcement canceled the raid, thank God, and the daycare continued to thrive over the next few years. The man who gave Randy the information began to attend the church, gave his heart to Christ, and became a faithful member during our time in Toccoa.

God blessed us beyond our dreams. Here we had our first encounter with the KKK and intense spiritual warfare. Life was difficult at times, but the good times far outweighed the difficult ones. Our pay increased. We purchased our first home. The church grew, and lives were changed. We fought financial battles, church bosses, and fights on our outreach buses. We performed marriages and baby dedications and honored and buried those who went into eternity. We became a part of our community and watched our church become very multiracial and multiethnic. During all of this, we were learning invaluable lessons that would serve us throughout our ministry. God continued weaving together the tapestry of our lives and the town of Toccoa.

Just a few months after moving, I found that I was expecting an addition to our family, and I was four months along! This pregnancy was quite scary for us because we had just taken a step of faith to pastor our small church. We had no insurance and no money. We refused to accept government assistance because we felt it would bring shame to our church as they could not afford to pay us enough. We had taken a significant pay cut to move to Georgia, and although I was working in our daycare, I had not yet been able to find a job teaching public school.

My second pregnancy was also without the complications my doctor had predicted. Labor and delivery progressed without a hitch—less than four hours, from the first contraction to her birth.

Jordan was nearly two years old when God gave us Danielle, who looked more like Randy than our first daughter. I told him that it just wasn't fair that I did most of the work to give those girls life, and they had the nerve to come out looking like him! Randy finally had two little ones who were blood relatives and who looked like him in so many ways. As they grew, they even began to display many of Randy's personality traits, which thrilled me to no end! When they misbehaved, I could always say, "She's your daughter, and you cannot deny her!" Randy loved being a girl dad, and he knew that God had healed more of his pain at being rejected with the birth of these two children. Whenever he walked into the room, their faces lit up, and in return, he adored them. They loved him and accepted him because he was their father, their playmate, and because they sensed his deep love for them.

||||||||||||||||||||||||||||||||||||||||||||||||||||||||||||||||||||||||||||||||||||||

Jordan and Danielle loved
Randy and accepted him
because he was their father,
their playmate, and because they
sensed his deep love for them.

We had purchased our first home during this time, finding that it was cheaper to buy and pay a mortgage than rent a house. This house was nestled in a cul-de-sac at the bottom of a hill, and Randy discovered that a little red wagon carrying a 2-year-old child and a 24-year-old man would speed down that hill. It went faster in the snow. It went even faster when a 2-year-old, a 4-year-old, and a 26-year-old man rode in the little red wagon. Often, on snow days, people from the church would arrive at our house to ride that little red wagon or flying saucers down the icy hill in front of our house. In Randy's mind, it was a recipe for a party, and the more who came, the better the party. He was always ready to invite people to church, and those invitations often overflowed into invitations to our home. Randy did learn toward the end of his life that I needed to be consulted before he gave open, impromptu invitations.

The second Christmas in our new home, Randy decided that we would have a Christmas party. The church had grown substantially. We were being paid more and could finally afford to give back to the church people. He wanted it to be a fun night with lots of people in attendance. Sunday night came, and he announced that everyone in attendance was welcome to drop into our home for some finger foods and eggnog after service. EVERYONE. If they were there at the service and didn't come to our house, we would be greatly offended. I am still unsure as to where he got that particular idea, but, of course, no one wanted to offend their pastor and his family, so they came. And kept coming. And kept coming.

The entire cul-de-sac was full of cars that were double-parked, cars that went up the hill, and cars that were parked on adjoining roads. There were people in the house that night that I had never seen before. I am not so sure they even attended our church service that night! But we were not offended. There was no chance. Over 115 people came to our home that night. I ran out of food, I ran out of eggnog, and I was begging God to somehow multiply for me the way he did the two fishes and five loaves of bread. Instead of doing that, he helped people understand that they needed to leave when the food was gone. I think it took me a week to get spilled food and drinks out of my furniture and off the floors, but oh, what wonderful memories we had of that night.

The weaving continued.

We were beginning to outgrow the church building, needed more space, and made plans to build a new sanctuary and offices. We began to add pastoral staff to our team and, unfortunately, also subtract a few. Randy learned that some people who God called into ministry were not necessarily called onto OUR ministry team. Randy had been allowed to be adopted into a wonderful family, and he desired to adopt people into our staff family and make them a part of our lives. Sometimes, this didn't work. He also had to learn that just because a person could not follow through with their calling did not mean they were rejecting him. When a staff member failed, Randy felt as if he had also failed. It was very personal to him, and as a shepherd, he grieved intensely over ministry failures. Someone once said not to take things like this personally, but to Randy, it truly felt personal. Growing pains are never easy.

||||||||||||||||||||||||||||||||||||||||||||||||||||||||||||||||||||||||||||||||||||

Growing pains are never easy.

A young man who began attending the church wanted to do something significant for the building program. We thought he had both the income and the resources to do so. One Sunday morning, he privately handed Randy a post-dated check for $100,000. He told Randy that he wanted it to be the seed money for building the new sanctuary, which had a projected cost of $700,000. What a faith-builder!

The gift of this check became the impetus to proceed with the ground-breaking and pursue permanent financing. Approximately six weeks into building the sanctuary, a tornado came through Toccoa, hit our church, destroyed the new facility, and caused major damage to the existing structures. Fortunately, although the daycare and the offices were occupied, no one on our property was injured. However, during clean-up from the storm, Randy forgot that tennis shoes are not the best deterrent to nails, and when he stepped on a broken board, the nail that was in the board went all the way through his foot. A tetanus shot, not Randy's favorite thing to have, was administered. We purchased boots for the remainder of the clean-up. We began building again, and although there were many delays and problems with the construction, we were in the new sanctuary within seven months. It was the largest church building in the town and became a venue for community events.

Oh, and the $100,000 check? It bounced. Randy and I, the church board, and the building committee were all appalled. Still, we accepted that God used that young man to encourage us to proceed with what God called the church to do—construct a larger building that would house more people who needed to hear the gospel of Jesus Christ. We did not know it at the time, but God was weaving more life experiences into our tapestry that would set the threads for a more incredible picture in the future.

We thought our family was complete until we began to wish for another addition. Since Randy was adopted, we discussed the possibility of adopting a child who needed a family. We put that idea to rest when we found that I was pregnant! When our two daughters were seven and nine years old, God blessed us with another daughter, Alayna.

This pregnancy was different from my previous two. I don't know if it was God preparing me for a difficult road ahead or if some sense of spiritual knowledge knew my body was not doing what it was supposed to do. The doctor dismissed my concerns and stated that since I was older, thirty-three at the time, and since this was the third pregnancy, I might face some problems. Randy and I prayed fervently that this would not be the case.

Based on the size of this baby, I had three different due dates, and the doctor was quite puzzled that the baby did not seem to be growing according to the scale. Eight weeks before my last due date, I went for a check-up only to discover I had a severe kidney and bladder infection. Blood work also revealed that my thyroid hormones were unbalanced. I began antibiotics and promised more testing but went into preterm labor that afternoon. Since one of my due dates was two weeks later, the doctor decided to allow the labor to progress and see if my contractions stopped. They did not. I labored through the next afternoon when the doctor decided to break my water and put me on a Pitocin drip to speed the labor.

I proved to Randy that I was a strong, stalwart woman who could labor and deliver a baby while drugged with Pitocin and without an epidural. He had invited friends to come and visit while I was in labor, and I finally had to inform the nursing staff that no one else was welcome! Randy, the original party man, had mistakenly thought it was party time and that the labor was going to be a quick process. During the long hours of labor, he repeatedly said to me, "Baby, we can do this!" I finally grabbed him by the neckline of his shirt, pulled his face into mine, and growled, "We are not doing this. I am. Now, get me some drugs." He gently removed my hands from his shirt, told me that he, as the labor coach, was in charge, and proceeded to call the nurse for an epidural. It was too late to administer the epidural. Twenty-six hours of labor and delivery gave us another beautiful baby girl.

When Alayna was born, she was in distress. She was a "blue baby." She had been without oxygen for too long, and the doctors were unsure if she would live. Her birth weight was lower than expected, 5 pounds 6 ounces, and she struggled to breathe. They swiftly took her from the room to do life-saving measures. I was unable to see or hold her in those first few minutes. Over the next few hours, Randy and I prayed, begging God to let her live. I wondered why my body had betrayed me in such a manner. We did not know that God was orchestrating circumstances to deepen our relationship with him.

I was dismissed from the hospital the next day, but Alayna was still gravely ill, so I left the hospital without my baby. That was one of the most difficult moments of my life. Randy took me home to rest before he went back to the church to pray. Alayna's oxygen levels were dangerously low by the afternoon, and she struggled to take tiny breaths. Randy received an emergency call to return to the hospital. They told him that she would need to be sent to a hospital with a neonatal unit or die. With his approval, the hospital staff began to search for a bed for our tiny preemie and finally found a place for her at Eggleston Children's Hospital in Atlanta.

As Randy drove to our home, he passed a graveyard close to our house where Satan attacked his mind, telling him that our precious daughter would die, and it would be necessary for him to explain to our church why God had not healed her. He later told me that, in his mind, he saw a small casket and our family standing next to it to receive family and friends. How could he be a pastor, filled with faith, but lose an infant daughter to death? Randy's potential to be opinionated and strong-willed, to dig into what was important to us, kicked into Randy's heart and spirit in full force. He parked the car to get out and walk in the graveyard. At that moment, he conversed with the enemy of his soul, "Satan, I don't care what you say. I will believe God and believe that He will heal my baby. But if He does not, Jelly and I will still live for Him and will declare the works of the Lord!"

Randy then got back into his car and drove to our home to tell me the latest news about our baby girl. We went to the hospital to see her before they took her by ambulance to Atlanta, and we prayed over her one more time. Until that moment, I had not been allowed to touch her or bond with her. The entire experience seemed surreal as I wept over my precious newborn.

Randy and I followed the ambulance to Atlanta. During the trip, we prayed that she would remain stable in the ambulance and would live until they could get her to Eggleston Hospital and placed on life-support. Hours later, when we walked into the neonatal intensive care unit, I heard the beeps of machines, watched babies in distress, and saw little chests rising and falling to the tempo of ventilators. The only crying I could hear was that of parents who did not know if their babies were going to live or die or were already dying. I was part of that group.

As I stood over Alayna's bed, I began to sing to her through my tears. I sang a song entitled "He's Been Faithful," and it became my statement of faith. Regardless of what came, I knew that God's Word was true, and He would remain faithful through all of life's circumstances. As I sang to her, Randy held my hand, stood back, and wept.

We both knew that whatever might come, God would remain by our sides and comfort and love us through the coming days.

||||||||||||||||||||||||||||||||||||||||||||||||||||||||||||||||||||||||||||||||||

We both knew that whatever might come, God would remain by our sides and comfort and love us through the coming days.

Over the next few days, the doctors gave us updates as much as possible, and I rarely left the NICU. The reports were extremely difficult to hear: Due to her traumatic birth, she would probably be blind. She would be deaf and have learning disabilities and breathing issues all her life. At one point, Alayna worsened, and the doctors asked for permission to put her on an oscillator, an experimental machine at the time. Randy asked for one night to pray before making the decision, and the doctor consented.

During that night, Randy and I, again, committed Alayna's life to the Lord and stated our determination to live for Him, regardless of the future. Unbeknownst to us, two of our dear friends, Johnny and Stan, had come to Atlanta overnight to stay in the hotel room above us, joining their prayers and their faith with ours. The following day, they called to tell us they wanted to eat breakfast with us and then proceed to the hospital. As we walked through the door of the NICU, unsure of what to expect, the doctor walked toward us, shaking his head in disbelief. Fear tried to grip our hearts. We did not know what to anticipate until the doctor smiled. He said,

"I really don't know what happened, but there was a change over-night. Your baby does not need the oscillator. She does not need the ventilator. She does not even need the NICU. We are taking her off life-support and moving her to a regular room. She will probably go home with you in a few days." Happy dances happened right then and there!

Although she was a tiny baby, had lost weight in the hospital to under five pounds, and was considered "failure to thrive," Alayna progressed much more quickly than expected. Neither her mind nor her body suffered long-term effects from the trauma.

Randy, when he was twelve years old, began developing his faith walk at the birth of his youngest brother. That walk of faith came full circle as he had now believed God for miracles with his own child. The woven tapestry of faith and action continued as we walked out our desire to live and work for Him.

|||||||||||||||||||||||||||||||||||||||||||||||||||||||||||||||||||||||||||||||||||||||

Randy's walk of faith came full
circle as he had now believed God
for miracles with his own child.

We dearly loved our time in this mountain setting and the people of the area. We made so many friends in our town and had seen God change lives that others thought could never be changed. In October of 1992, as I listened to the mayor give Randy the key to the city, declaring it Randy Valimont Day, I heard the voice of God in my spirit as He told me that He was calling us away from Toccoa.

Unbeknownst to me, at the same time, God was also speaking to Randy. This would be our last Pastor's Appreciation Day in Toccoa.

GRIFFIN, GEORGIA

Over the next few months, opportunities abounded for us to move to different churches. We received calls from various towns and from out of state, but nothing felt right until April when we received a call from a board member at Griffin First Assembly of God asking us to consider moving to Griffin, Georgia. We visited the church and felt that this was the right thing to do. Within a few short weeks, we packed our growing family and all our possessions into moving trucks and moved to Griffin. There, we saw God weave another substantial part of the tapestry of our lives. Slowly but surely, we began to see a picture of God's grace and goodness emerge.

Upon leaving Toccoa, the Lord reminded Randy of the scripture He had given him before we arrived in Toccoa:

So they got up early in the morning and went out into the Wilderness of Tekoa; and as they went out, Jehoshaphat stood and said, "Hear me, O Judah, and you inhabitants of Jerusalem! Believe and trust in the Lord your God and you will be established (secure). Believe and trust in His prophets and succeed."
—2 Chronicles 20:20 (author paraphrase)

Without a doubt, God had spoken to us in 1984. Our wilderness of Toccoa had grown, and now a new highway connected it to the towns directly south of us. Nine years before, what had seemed a wilderness was no longer remote or cut off from other areas. We had believed and trusted in the Lord during our time in that beautiful mountain town. We learned to live a life of faith and sacrifice, fully foolish enough to take God at His "Word" and to secure us where He wanted us to be established. As a result of our belief and trust in a God who never fails, we had succeeded in what God had us to do for that time. We made many mistakes, but we always depended on God to help us navigate the issues we created and even those that were created by others.

An increase in our finances or the size of a church was never a consideration when Randy and I contemplated making a change. Any move we considered was predicated on the question of what we felt God wanted us to do and what was in His divine plan. In fact, it was often the exact opposite: we took a pay cut to make a move! It was the same for our move to Griffin. The church in Toccoa and the one in Griffin were about the same size, and the pay package in Griffin was somewhat less as the cost of living was much higher. We knew that if God wanted us there, He would provide. He had proven to us repeatedly that He was faithful, and He would not fail us. We had stood on Psalm 37:25 (NIV) all our married lives and would continue to do so:

> *"I was young and now I am old, yet I have never seen the*
> *righteous forsaken or their children begging bread."*

The church in Griffin immediately began to grow, and this previously reputed "preacher-killing church" became Randy's heartbeat. He loved the people, the staff, the town, and the ministry he was allowed to develop. Within a few short months, the church had a mighty revival. We began to see drug addicts, prostitutes, thieves, adulterers, and other truly godless people come in from the streets to seek a relationship with Jesus. Broken homes began to be put back together. Church finances increased. A bus ministry was begun to bring in children from indigent areas, so they could hear the gospel of Jesus Christ. The previously all-white church became fully integrated as people from twenty-six nations of the world began to attend. The church became what Randy envisioned as a young teen, a "whosoever will" church. He wanted whoever came through the doors of the church to be welcomed by everyone. In addition, he wanted all to feel the love of Christ in the congregants. They did.

One day, two young men walked into Randy's office to give him a tithe check and told him that it was their first honest tithe to the Lord. Randy was a bit confused as their previous tithes had been quite large. The young men explained that they had heard a message Randy preached about the blessings of the tither. They figured if they tithed on their income, God would bless them. The problem was that their income came from the sale of marijuana which they illegally grew locally. They had been tithing on their marijuana sales.

They had been caught, they told Randy, with the largest marijuana crop ever found in the state of Georgia at that time. Did God bless the crop, or was the real blessing that the government caught them? They took responsibility for their crimes but served no time for their misdeeds. The tithe check they gave to Randy was from a business they had started, and it was honest labor, not connected to their former drug trade. They understood the principle of tithing even if they were originally misguided in their attempts to receive the blessings of the tither.

It did not matter who wanted to be a part of Griffin First Assembly. Randy felt that if God could use him, God could use anyone. The rejection that Randy had felt from an early age became less of a deterrent in Randy's heart. He began to feel more accepted as he allowed God to use him to help change the face of a church and a city. He began to understand that the Lord had ordered his life, and God had brought him into this place to do a specific task for a particular season. We had no idea what would unfold in our lives over the next few years. The tapestry that God had begun to weave was suddenly taking form at such a fast rate that we could barely keep up.

|||||||||||||||||||||||||||||||||||||||||||||||||||||||||||||||||||||||||||||

> The tapestry that God had begun to weave was suddenly taking form at such a fast rate that we could barely keep up.

Two things became a prominent part of Randy's life after we moved to Griffin. Although he still dealt with feelings of rejection, he wanted others to feel accepted on every level. It did not seem to matter if someone failed him, failed in their Christian life, or failed in their personal life. Randy wanted them to feel that once their failure was behind them, they could still succeed. He ended many of his conversations with people by telling them he was proud of them. To many, it was the first time they had heard those words. Randy wanted people to know that they could and would do better than they were doing. He believed in people and in their desire to live and work for God. It was almost as if he were provoking others to good works with his words of affirmation and encouragement. He knew how much it meant to his own heart for someone to be pleased with him and proud of the work he was doing. As a result, he took that need and filled it for others.

Randy's acceptance of people caused him to open his heart, his arms, and our home to people, especially young adults who had no close family. He invited many into our home for holidays because he never wanted anyone to spend them alone. Once again, skin color and ethnicity did not matter. They became our "adopted children." Many that we "adopted" stayed a part of our lives, often calling from various parts of the world to check on our family and the church's ministries. If they were in town, they were always welcome.

Many times, I would wake up on Thanksgiving morning or Randy would call on the way home from our Easter services and say, "Oh, by the way, we have a few more coming for lunch. I know you will have enough. You always do." Yes, I would often panic!

Holidays were important for our immediate family and church family. I made it a practice to put out the word that if anyone would be alone for a holiday, they should call me and let me know they were coming, so I could make more food. That way, I could get the jump on Randy's impromptu invitations. Frequently, I would go over my guest list just before people began to arrive and, again, assess the numbers to assure myself that I had enough food. Most of the time, I was surprised as more than I anticipated arrived hungry. However, we never ran out of food. Randy was in his element as he entertained everyone with stories. Laughter was always present, along with too much food.

Inevitably, before the meal was over, Randy would become reflective and begin to ask our young guests, "What did you learn today?" Many times, the time spent together turned into mentoring sessions for our guests as Randy poured his knowledge, guidance, and concern into their lives. Loving and accepting people was a desire deep in Randy's heart. His heart compelled him to assure people that they knew it. The love and acceptance he experienced in his life helped him meet and accept people where they were, with few reservations.

||||||||||||||||||||||||||||||||||||||||||||||||||||||||||||||||||||||||||||||||||||||||

Loving and accepting people was a desire deep in Randy's heart.

In 1998, Jordan, our oldest daughter, became seriously ill. Over a period of six months, Jordan was in and out of emergency rooms and hospitals with gastrointestinal issues. Diagnostic tests were inconclusive, and her pain was intense. Doctors did not know what to do. We had exhausted all avenues to find answers. Jordan lost weight, was very weak, and had to be placed in a home-bound learning environment.

After a tough week, I asked Randy if he had ever considered the possibility of a genetic link to an unknown disease. I was desperate! I knew my family's medical history, but Randy did not know his genetic predispositions or illnesses. The previously disclosed information in his birth records was vague. His birth and adoption records had given no medical information to him. Lack of information is one of the problems that children of closed adoptions may one day face; they have no genetic or medical history. There was nothing to write on official forms that asked for maternal and paternal medical conditions. There were no clues about elusive medical or mental issues.

Due to Jordan's intense illness, Randy decided to begin the research process to see if he could discover a possible genetic issue or a medical history. Although the medical records and disclosure were to protect the birth parents, in that era, it seemed that no one thought that certain disclosures were needed to protect the child.

Randy wrote to the department of vital records to obtain a copy of his original birth certificate. When the information arrived, he was appalled to find that they redacted most of the identifying information. The only information available to him was his adoptive name, birth hospital, date, time of birth, and weight at birth. They gave him the ages of his birth parents: thirty-three and thirty-four. Although they provided no medical information, he knew immediately in his heart that he was the product of an affair. He did not want to go any further in his search for answers. It was enough that he now knew part of the reason they put him up for adoption.

Jordan worsened, and through prayer and more research, I found that her illness was due to a medication that she had been given over an eighteen-month period. A local pharmacist and friend confirmed this, and the doctors immediately removed her from the drug. The medication was stored in her liver, causing severe pain and compromising her health. Over the following months, as the medication slowly worked its way out of her liver, she fully recovered.

I do not know what other circumstances would have encouraged Randy to seek answers about his biological family. I am not suggesting that God caused Jordan's illness, but I am sure that God USED this difficult circumstance to continue a process of understanding the destiny of God, a work that He was weaving to present a beautiful tapestry of life, just as He uses all circumstances, good and bad, to work for our good.

||||||||||||||||||||||||||||||||||||||||||||||||||||||||||||||||||||||||||||||

> I am sure that God used Jordan's illness to continue ... a work that He was weaving to present a beautiful tapestry of life, just as He uses all circumstances, good and bad, to work for our good.

Romans 8:28 (KJV) says,

"For we know that all things work together for those who love the Lord and are called according to his purpose."

Although we did not understand it at the time, God was certainly working things together for our good, taking uncomfortable circumstances and using them for HIS purpose.

THE SHADOW OF A PICTURE BEGINS TO EMERGE: FINDING ANSWERS

Throughout the years of life and ministry, Randy had seen so many family separation/adoption reunions that did not go well. They were often a nightmare from beginning to end and rarely turned out to be a positive experience. Randy had been raised in a good home with excellent parents and two brothers that he deeply loved. He was loyal to that family and never wanted to do anything to bring pain to them. Yet, once he began the process of finding biological information, it made him realize that there were questions that needed answers and a sense of understanding that he needed to be healthy and whole.

Randy was not sure that he wanted to add a possibly traumatic experience to his life, but he asked me to find out whatever information I could about his birth family. However, he had no interest in meeting them. He feared, once again, being rejected.

I began to register Randy's birth circumstances on adoption reunion websites. Whenever I found another website, I would register his information and wait to hear from someone, anyone who might possibly be a part of his birth family. No one answered any query. I came to a place where I had no answers and nowhere else to turn without delving deeply into the possibility of a personal encounter with the birth family. I'd reached the proverbial impasse.

For some reason, during a discussion late one night, Randy suddenly decided that there had to be more to his story, and he wanted to know everything. He told me that he wanted me to actively pursue answers and do more than just register on websites. Maybe God had a plan for him to meet his birth family and let them know that they had made a good decision to give him to Norman and June Valimont. Maybe, since there had to be more to the story, there was more than life at stake. Maybe eternity.

A few days later, I called the attorney who had handled the adoption in 1960. When the paperwork for the adoption had been given to June and Norman, the attorney told them that whenever Randy was an adult, his records would be opened to him. We thought that maybe this was the time to open the records, so Randy would have the answers he desired. Surprisingly, the attorney, who had become quite elderly, answered the telephone and told me he was in the process of closing his practice. If I had only called two weeks previous, he would have been happy to share the information with me; however, all his private records had been shredded the week before, and he could not remember the details of the adoption. There was no one left in the office who had been present for the adoption, and no one that he knew could be forthcoming with the answers. It seemed that the information was totally lost.

During the next two years, I continued to search adoption reunion websites looking for possible connections but found nothing. I continued to register on various pages, thinking that if someone did want to know about Randy one day, they could easily find him. At that time, neither Randy nor I knew that his birth mother had told her children and extended family that her baby had died. His birth father had never acknowledged that there was a baby and never told anyone about him. No one was looking for Randy, and those who knew anything were not telling.

Not knowing the answers to his medical history and the circumstances around his birth began to trouble Randy. One of the things that is interesting to note is that very often medical issues or predispositions to medical issues do not show up early in life. It is only as we age that we develop high blood pressure, diabetes, heart disease, cholesterol problems, and other age-related medical issues. When a child is given up for adoption, the birth parents often do not have medical issues to disclose. In Randy's case, it was not only an issue with disclosure but a lack of knowledge. Randy was getting older and began to wonder if there were potential medical problems for which he needed to be aware. Although Jordan was now well, would there be another disease that he or his children inherited that would suddenly be discovered in his or their bodies?

By the end of the year 2000, Randy decided to pursue more answers. Through a friend, we found a private investigator that specialized in adoption answers. He called her, hired her, and received the promise that if she could find no answers to his questions that he would pay nothing for her services. Within a few short weeks, we had some of the answers to questions that had plagued Randy for years. Years of searching and registering on web pages came to a quick end when a professional became involved!

As we spoke with the investigator, I asked her how she had so quickly found the answers we needed. She stated, "Jelly, when you need brain surgery, you call a brain surgeon. When you need the house painted, you call a painter. When you need hidden answers, you call someone who specializes in finding the truth: a private investigator. This is my specialty, and it is what I do!" I am so grateful that her skills of research far surpassed my dallying on reunion websites. She knew exactly where to go and the questions to ask, and the information was quickly forthcoming.

She gave us a few answers as we spoke on the telephone, but the remaining answers would be in her report. She also told us that just because she had identifying information about his birth mother, we should not expect his birth mother's husband to be his birth father. She was correct! After fees were paid to the private investigator, she sent the maternal information, letting us know that it was very possible that we could learn more after a conversation with the birth mother, should we choose to contact her. She also cautioned us that it was very possible his birth mother would share nothing and would deny everything. If Randy called her, it was very possible that his birth mother would—once again—reject him.

This is the information the investigator shared with us:

At the time of Randy's birth, Marion, his birth mother, was a 33-year-old, full-blooded German woman who had given birth to a total of six children, including Randy. Four were older than Randy. After Randy was born, she gave birth to another child. One baby was given up for adoption, and one had died in adulthood of a congenital heart issue. His birth mother was still alive and lived in the same town where Randy had been born. The private investigator provided Marion's current telephone number and address. However, her husband was not listed as being Randy's biological father. The only way to get that information was to call and speak with her and see if she would divulge the information he sought.

During the years of not having answers, Randy had tried not to imagine the circumstances of his birth. He assumed that his parents were probably teenagers or that he was the product of an affair. He had seen both scenarios in the lives of people he had known: Someone was immoral and gave birth to an illegitimate child that they did not want to keep. They wanted to disregard their sinfulness, forget the child, and pretend it never happened. In his mind, he was given away and never thought about again.

I argued with Randy that what he was thinking was often very far from the truth. I have seen women grieve the loss of a child for many years, often until their own death. That loss could be from abortion, miscarriage, stillborn birth, voluntarily giving a child up for adoption, termination of parental rights, or even because of kidnapping. A woman never forgets a child she has conceived. She never forgets the child or the pain of not having that child in her life. That child may be remembered with love and heartache. It may be remembered as a burden. The loss could even be remembered as a relief. But it is remembered.

I explained to Randy that as she aged, his birth mother needed to know that she had done the right thing: Randy had a good life, he had been adopted by parents who desperately loved him, and he was serving God in ministry as a pastor. He needed to share the gospel of Jesus Christ with her and give her an opportunity to know Christ. In addition, she needed closure for that time of her life. She especially needed to know before she went into eternity, and his opportunity to get answers was gone forever. In my opinion, if Randy wanted answers, he needed to move toward finding them before it was too late.

‖‖

> I explained to Randy that as she aged, his birth mother needed to know that she had done the right thing.

Within a few days of receiving the information from the private investigator, Randy decided he would make the call to Marion to see if she would talk to him about the circumstances surrounding his birth. He knew that he would need to be cautious and sensitive to the emotions that he might dredge up after more than forty years of secrecy. Years of ministry had equipped him to be sensitive when helping others divulge a secret, either purposefully or accidentally!

Randy and I sat in his office using a speakerphone as he made the call to Marion. She answered on the second ring, and the conversation unfolded. When Randy identified himself, she very emotionally stated, "Oh, I have been waiting on your call!" Giving her a moment to compose herself, we heard her say through her tears to someone else in the room, "It's my son. The one I gave up for adoption." She had never ceased to think of Randy as her son or the fact that he was not a part of her life.

Due to the laws in 1960, she had been unable to find who had adopted him, if the family had been a good family, where he had lived, if he had been happy or unhappy, or how his life had unfolded. I don't know if she ever tried or if she walked away and never looked back. I do know that she never acknowledged to her family that he was alive somewhere. If she had ever admitted that she gave up Randy for adoption, she would have had to admit the reason: immorality. She was unwilling to do that or to open the door for her other children to possibly seek out their brother. Had they sought out their brother, it would have been necessary for her to give her reasons or her excuses.

After she composed herself, Marion quickly followed up with the question, "What color are you?" This question was a shock and led to many more questions: Why would she ask that question? Am I white? Am I brown? Am I black? What am I really? Who IS my birth father? For the first time in his life, Randy felt the sting of prejudice, especially when his birth mother stated that this was one of the reasons he was given for adoption.

It was then that Randy learned that he was not of Italian descent but of Iranian descent. When he spoke with Marion, it was the spring of 2002, and with the recent World Trade Center attacks, it was not a good time in history to be associated with the Iranian culture. The mere fact that he was part Iranian was somewhat disconcerting for him. According to Marion, his birth father was a very dark man, so much so that one of the reasons Marion consented to give Randy up for adoption was because of the possibility that his skin color would be very dark and so different from that of her other children. He would be a constant reminder to her and everyone else that she had been unfaithful to her husband.

Marion and her husband had reconciled after Randy's birth, and they had had another child, but Marion spent more than forty years waiting on the call to confirm that she had made the right decision. Her question about his skin color was probably another plea from her heart to confirm it. During the call, Marion expressed to Randy that both she and her husband had come to know Christ. She was ecstatic to know that not only was Randy a Christ-follower, but he was also a minister of the gospel of Jesus Christ.

A short time later, Randy and I made a trip to New York to meet his birth mother and two of his birth siblings. Two other siblings were living in Florida, and they later traveled to Griffin to meet him. His maternal birth siblings had all been told for years that the baby she birthed in 1960 (Randy) had died shortly after he was born. One sister had suspected the lie and, for many years, had anticipated finding the truth.

On that trip to New York, Randy discovered the name of his birth father, some of the details of the affair they had, and why he had been given up for adoption. Randy also met Marion's husband, with whom she had reconciled and remained through the years. Upon meeting him, he looked at Randy and stated, "I told her to abort you, so she would never have to deal with this again." The anger this man had toward his wife, her lover, and Randy was both palpable and painful. Again, rejection reared its ugly head.

All the "ifs" came into play in Randy's mind: If Marion had followed her husband's desires, if his birth father had not been called back to Iran to perform surgery on the wife of the Shah, if his return had not been delayed—if all these things had happened differently, another abortion could have been performed. Randy's tapestry would not have been woven, and many lives would not have had the opportunity to be affected by Randy's passion for God and by his life.

This information from Marion absolutely proved to Randy that God's hand was upon him before he was ever born, and God had a plan to use him. He believed Jeremiah 1:5 (NKJV), when it states (emphasis added),

"Before I formed you in the womb I knew you; *Before you were born* I sanctified you; I ordained you *a prophet to the nations.*"

God not only knew Randy, but He had a plan to use his life in supernatural ways.

‖‖‖

God not only knew Randy,
but He had a plan to use his
life in supernatural ways.

After the meeting with Marion, Randy and I began to process the information in our minds. We talked about the questions we had asked and the answers we had received. We had no reason to doubt her answers and knew that the answers had also provided understanding as to who Randy was. Finally, knowing that he was of immigrant family roots helped him grasp one of the reasons he was so accepting of other people groups and cultures. He was American by birth but was also from two very distinct cultures that provided a new dimension to his life.

Randy had always loved German food and the German culture. He had attributed it to the fact that his grandparents were Russian-Polish, and there were many similarities in the cultures. However, upon finding that he was half-German, clarity dawned! His mission trips to Germany and the affinity he felt for the country were probably because he was truly genetically connected.

The love he had felt for the unknown people of Iran was because he was half Iranian. Throughout his travels into the Middle East, Randy had frequently been stopped by people who were from the area. They would begin speaking to him in Hebrew, Arabic, or Farsi, and he would quietly explain that he was not from the area but was American Italian. Many would look at him in disbelief, shake their heads, and walk away. They knew, but he did not! Randy had also played a major role in beginning the first Iranian Bible college and in producing the Iranian Fire Bible in the Farsi language. Until that moment, he had not known that his heart was drawn to his own biological family. The question of nature versus nurture arose, and Randy had more understanding of who he really was than he had ever known before.

During that one and only meeting with his birth mother, Marion never expressed regret for giving Randy up for adoption. She never said she was wrong to do so. There was never a close relationship that developed between the two of them, but Randy was finally able to get the answers he desired and discover a little about his birth father, including his name and place of residence.

Marion died in 2009, knowing that, although she had given up a child for adoption, she had also provided an answer to prayer for another childless couple. She did not know that through her actions, she helped set in motion something that would change the world for Jesus Christ and that before he died, Randy would lead one biological sister to Christ. God CAN work all things together for those who love Him and are called according to His purpose.

Another thread in the tapestry was woven into his frame, and God continued to make the picture interestingly beautiful. The destiny of God was becoming more and more clear as Randy began to understand how much his heavenly Father had done to ensure that His work would be completed.

I thank my God every time I remember you. In all my prayers for all of you, I always pray with joy because of your partnership in the gospel from the first day until now, being confident of this, that he who began a good work in you will carry it on to completion until the day of Christ Jesus.
—Philippians 1:3-6 (NIV)

CHAPTER 5

LIVING LIKE
A MIRACLE
WHEN YOU FEEL
LIKE A MESS

"The passion for acceptance and the pain of rejection are the reasons an adopted child will almost always, at some point, seek to find their birth parents. When they find them, the foremost questions they must ask are, 'Why did you give me up, forsake me, or reject me? What is wrong with me? Why did you not love me?' And no matter how rational the answers are, in most cases, there seems to be an abiding grief and a passion for acceptance."
—Rev. Gerald Jordan

Randy was no different than many children of adoption, wondering where he came from, why he was not wanted, why he was not good enough to be loved. He felt the same loss, grief, shame, rejection, low self-esteem, and identity issues as many adopted children. He spent many years trying to make himself feel good enough to love and make others love him. He could not understand why he didn't feel worthy of being loved or how anyone could possibly love him without knowing him. He had amazing coping skills for silencing the questions in his heart, but as mentioned previously, it was only at the birth of his baby brother, Raymond, that Randy truly understood that a person could love someone with whom they are not genetically connected.

Raymond's birth was a cataclysmic event in Randy's life. Not only did he instantly fall in love with Baby Raymond, but he finally understood that his adoptive family did love him as much as they said they did. They had already demonstrated their love for Randy, but the rejection he felt as an infant was so deeply rooted in his heart and his psyche that it took Raymond's birth to make him truly understand love. In fact, Randy felt that Raymond was God's gift to him, personally. The bond that was forged at the birth of Raymond continued all of Randy's life.

IIIIIIIIIIIIIIIIIIIIIIIIIIIIIIIIIIIIIIIIIIIIIIIIIIIIIIIIIIIIIIIIIIIIIIIIIIIIIIIIIIII

> The bond that was forged
> at the birth of Raymond
> continued all of Randy's life.

From his earliest recollections, Randy was told that God had a plan for his life. There was a destiny that needed to be fulfilled. It was a difficult leap for Randy to make because he often felt that he was a mistake, a mess that God could not use. However, it was through the circumstances of Randy's birth, his history, and finally knowing his history that God was able to weave a beautiful life story into a finished product for His glory. I firmly believe that we all have a destiny, and God wants to use us to our greatest capabilities and then equip us for more than our capabilities.

Randy often remarked to me that he could not believe that God would use him for a particular task. He asked, "How can God use me? People don't know where I came from or my circumstances!" He was often humbled and reflected on the human impossibility of God's work in his life. However, even with the insecurity in his own abilities, Randy's destiny was not only to be a pastor and a leader but to reach the world with the cause of Jesus Christ. He felt that there was always more to do, always more money to raise, always more trips to make to spread the gospel, and more people to send to an unsaved, dying world. If God would use him, he would work and strive to be available. Randy never measured what he had done in life, but he did measure how much more needed to be done, and how great was the unfinished task.

There comes a point in time when we all look at our lives and what we have or have not accomplished. We assess our bucket lists and wonder if we will ever put a checkmark on the things that we have not done. It is during this time that we can either accept or reject the circumstances we have encountered and everything those circumstances bring to us. If we accept the things that have happened in our lives, we can then decide what to do with those circumstances, how we can grow, and how we can make those things work for good and bring favor into our lives.

If we choose not to accept the circumstances or fight against them, we begin to walk toward anger and frustration. We also begin to ask the age-old questions: "Why?" "Why me?" "Why not someone else?" "What could I have done differently?" "What could someone else have done differently that would have changed my circumstances?" And the big question, "How could a God who claims to love me allow this to happen?"

There are no formulas, no exact answers to these questions. There is the knowledge that while circumstances are often unexpected and unexplainable, there is also a God who will walk us through the challenges, holding our hands and helping to weave what He sees in our future and through to the end of our lives.

You see, life is full of challenges, twists, and turns that we all face. Throughout biblical history, we find stories of people who seemed to think they were headed for a certain place only to find that their journey was changed, a detour was taken, and life did not progress down a straight, uneventful road. Randy's life, his journey, was much like this with surprises and unexpected, unanticipated events.

||||||||||||||||||||||||||||||||||||||||||||||||||||||||||||||||||||||||||||||||||||

> Although we do not know
> what the plan may be, God
> always has a perfect plan, a
> plan that He's designed.

Although we do not know what the plan may be, God always has a perfect plan, a plan that He's designed. Unfortunately, mankind will often cause trouble with those plans. When mankind creates disorder with God's plans, it is not the end. God has an alternate plan. When Randy's birth mother and father became involved with one another, it was not God's plan. His plan was that they would both live pure and holy lives, but they made a choice not to do so. When a child resulted from that union, God had another plan, both for the parents and for the child that resulted from their immorality. It was not the original plan, but it was also not the end when the plan was thwarted. God took what had begun in sin, and although Randy thought he was a mistake, God used him for untold eternal significance.

In Genesis, the story of the beginning of creation and mankind is told. The Garden of Eden must have been a beautiful place, filled with everything man could possibly ever need. God had a perfect plan, but Adam and Eve thwarted that plan by listening to Satan, and they botched, messed up, and interrupted God's plan; however, God did not destroy mankind for the mistake. He simply implemented another plan, an alternate one, a plan that would bring mankind back into fellowship with their Father and let them be free from sin.

In 1 Samuel 16, we find part of the story of David, the youngest son of Jesse. In many ways, David was rejected by his own family. He was the son of a concubine and was not as valued as one of Jesse's legitimate sons. He was often sent into the fields to work with the sheep, a job reserved for servants, not sons. He was often excluded from family activities.

The prophet Samuel was sent by God to Jesse's home to anoint another king. He knew that one of Jesse's sons had been chosen by God, but Samuel did not know which one had been chosen. He called them all to the sacrifice, knowing that God would tell him which was to be king. First Samuel 16:4-5 (NIV) describes the situation:

Samuel did what the Lord said. When he arrived at
Bethlehem, the elders of the town trembled when they
met him. They asked, "Do you come in peace?"
Samuel replied, "Yes, in peace; I have come to sacrifice to the Lord.
Consecrate yourselves and come to the sacrifice with me." Then he
consecrated Jesse and his sons and invited them to the sacrifice.

In this scripture, notice that Jesse and his sons were invited to the sacrifice, but later scripture reveals that although the prophet Samuel invited them all, David did not get the invitation. He was left in the fields, taking care of the sheep, again, a job that was normally relegated to servants, not sons.

All of Jesse's sons walked past the prophet, as instructed, but not one of those present was chosen. It was only after the prophet Samuel asked if all the sons were present that Jesse admitted that there was one more son left in the fields: David. When David was called to come in from the fields, his own brother, Eliab, questioned why he was there, and who was tending the sheep. Eliab dismissed David's importance at the event.

When David appeared, God opened the eyes of the prophet Samuel to see who David would be one day. David was discounted by his father and his siblings, and it took a prophet anointed by God to show them David's destiny. Others may dismiss you and discount you and your life, but you count with God, you are important, and God has a destiny for you.

God can find you when everyone else discounts you and your life. When others dismiss you, remember that God has a destiny for you. When others try to destroy your dream, remember that God has the ability to restore, regardless of circumstances.

|||||||||||||||||||||||||||||||||||||||||||||||||||||||||||||||||||||||||||||||||||

God can find you when everyone else discounts you and your life.

People make mistakes and bad judgments. We sometimes miss what God has in store for us because we do not understand or do not follow what God has intended for us to do.

A bad judgment, a mistake, a mess that is seemingly made of one's life is not the end. It may be a thread that was not originally intended to be woven into the final tapestry, but God uses that thread and allows it to stay to provide greater dimension and add another layer to the finished project.

Fotouhi Ancestors: Randy's biological father
is second from the right, bottom row.

Valimont Family: Alayna, Danielle,
Jordan, Jelly and Randy 2002.

Alayna, Jordan and Danielle

Fotouhi welcome lunch July 2015

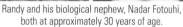

Griffin First Assembly Welcome 2015

Randy and his biological nephew, Nadar Fotouhi,
both at approximately 30 years of age.

Jaeli, our granddaughter, helping Randy tell the Christmas story, 2015.

The Valimont brothers: Jeff, Randy, Ray 1975

Jelly and Randy, Sadie Hawkins Day 1978

Jelly and Randy 2015

Randy's parents, June and Norman Valimont.

Randy and his biological father 2015

Randy and his biological sister, Suzanne Gavazzi.

Randy and our grandson, Shiloh, teaching leadership lessons to the pastoral staff at Griffin First Assembly.

Randy on the Sea of Galilee 2017

Randy at 6 months old.

The Valimont family: Randy, Jeff, June, Norman, Ray 1972

Randy, Rev. Fred Richards and Ray 1979

Randy, in his happy place, a Fire Bible event, Pebble Beach Golf Course 2019.

Randy meeting his paternal biological family in Atlanta 2015.

First meeting with the biological paternal family in Atlanta: Parvine (sister-in-law) Randy, Niloo (sister), Eric (nephew), Mohammed (brother).

Jelly and Randy 2011

CHAPTER 6

THE DESIGN EMERGES

Stories from the Threads

MARION'S STORY

Once Randy made the initial call to Marion, she was insistent that we come to meet her, especially when she heard that Randy was a minister of the gospel. In addition, Randy wanted to see her face, determine if there were any unknown bonds, and ask questions to her face. He had a great ability to see truth and untruth in the faces of people. He felt that if he could talk with her face-to-face, he would know if she were being truthful. In just a few short weeks, we traveled to New York and met with Marion and her husband in their home.

It was a slightly awkward meeting as her husband was not very happy that Randy even existed. In his words, if he'd had his way about it, Randy would not be alive. To understand his perspective, Marion's husband felt that she had rejected him. As her husband, he was not enough for her during a painful time in their marriage.

(Again, the grace of God was in action to even ensure that Randy would be born and that he would have a divine call on his life.) To Marion's husband, Randy was a reminder of a time in their marriage when his wife had been unfaithful to their marriage vows and had conceived a child, maybe more than once. However, Randy was the only child who survived.

This was not a long meeting but was very emotional for both Randy and Marion. During this time, Marion told us about all her other children, their ages when Randy was born, and where they were now living. Of the six children to whom she had given birth, five were still living, two of them in the same town. One son had been born with heart problems and had only lived until his late twenties. One daughter, her last child, had been born with special needs after a traumatic birth and was still living locally. After meeting with Marion, Randy and I also met two of his birth sisters and their families. They were all very welcoming and assured Randy that they wanted to be a part of his life, now that they knew he was a brother. However, circumstances, time, and distance did not allow for a close relationship between these maternal birth siblings to develop.

One person cannot repair overnight what has taken years to destroy, especially if the parties are unwilling to seek restoration.

Over time, we found that Marion expected Randy to be a catalyst that repaired broken relationships in her family, mainly because he was a minister and was supposed to have all the answers to their problems. Unfortunately, one person cannot repair overnight what has taken years to destroy, especially if the parties are unwilling to seek restoration. Only God can bring total restoration.

After we returned to Georgia, two other maternal birth siblings traveled to our home from Florida to meet the Valimont family. This meeting became one of the most important of Randy's life. It has been said that there is a strong genetic link between birth parents and their children, but it has also been suggested that the link between siblings is even greater. When Randy met Marion, there was not an immediate connection or a sense of finding what was missing in his life. However, the meetings with his birth siblings proved to be earthshaking for him.

Randy loved his Valimont family, but he felt that he needed more understanding of who he was and why he thought and felt the ways he did as he grew older and became a ministry leader. There were many great memories of his early life and his heart frequently reminded him of the fact that although someone did not want him, his Valimont parents did want him, loved him, and nurtured him throughout his life. He was very grateful for the home in which God had placed him. However, regardless of how much they tried to make him feel accepted and loved, he felt different. He thought differently and performed differently, thus widening a gap of questions regarding "who he really was" that had developed in his adult years.

Once Randy met the remaining two older siblings from his birth mother's side of the family, he began to understand some of his own personality traits. His older brother was a financial guru and had worked in the banking and investment business for many years. His sister Suzanne was strong-minded and competitive in the greatest sense of the word. She golfed—Randy's greatest, most loved sport.

When our children were growing up, I frequently stated to Randy that it would not hurt for him to allow them to occasionally win a game of checkers. His response was that if they were going to win, they needed to earn it! In our first conversation with Suzanne, she described how she was so competitive that she would not allow her children or grandchildren to win a game of checkers. They needed to earn it. It was then that we all understood how very strong genetics are in the lives of siblings. Randy also began to understand that two of his strongest personality traits, sound financial abilities and a strong sense of competition, came from his biological roots.

A strong relationship developed between Randy and these two birth siblings. He eventually had the great joy of leading Suzanne to Christ and watching her become a woman of God. This had been one of his prayers: that he would be allowed to share Christ with his birth family, and they would come to a saving knowledge of God's grace.

|||||||||||||||||||||||||||||||||||||||||||||||||||||||||||||||||||||||||||||||||||||

The threads of Randy's life were being pulled into place as God started to bring understanding to him. Some of the "tamping down" had been very painful—but necessary— to see the design emerge.

The tapestry was coming together, and a picture of God's plan and His grace was emerging. The threads of Randy's life were being pulled into place as God started to bring understanding to him. Some of the "tamping down" had been very painful—but necessary—to see the design emerge.

SUZANNE'S STORY

My brother Randy was such a blessing in my life, and because of him, I asked Jesus Christ into my heart, to become my Lord and Savior.

I was just a young girl when I found out that my mother was expecting a baby. Somehow, we knew that it was not the child of my biological father. When the baby was born, we were told that the baby had died. The truth was that the baby was put up for adoption, mainly because he was not my father's child. I always felt that the baby had lived (probably hearing aunts and cousins gossiping) and that it was a baby boy. I often wondered about him and what might have happened to him, how his life had transpired, who he was, and where he lived. I would sometimes look at strangers thinking that they looked like me.

In 2002, I received a phone call from my brother, Ken, saying that an unknown brother had contacted him looking for his bio-logical family. What an exciting time for me! I had been in Florida and was leaving shortly thereafter to return to New York, where I lived during the summertime. My husband and I decided to stop on our way home to meet my brother.

We decided to meet Randy at a nearby motel in Griffin, Georgia. I first laid eyes on Randy as he walked down the hallway, and the feeling of seeing him for the first time was surreal. We spent the evening and the next morning talking about our lives. Randy asked questions about his biological parents, and I answered to the best of my ability.

From that point, Randy and I had a very special relationship. We made up for lost years, and it felt as if we had grown up together. We also discovered how very much we were alike. The sibling bond between us was very strong, and his family would often laugh at how similar we were.

One of the passions that Randy and I shared was the game of golf. Over the years, we traveled to some world-famous golf courses to play in tournaments in which he was involved to raise money for missions—another of his passions.

In 2014, Randy invited me to go to Calcutta, India, with him and my niece, Danielle. It was the 50th-anniversary celebration for Calcutta Mercy Ministries, founded by Mark and Huldah Buntain. Randy was the current president of the ministry, and I was honored to be a part of the celebration. As I participated in the activities, I was so proud of my brother and his daughter Danielle and so honored to see the work that they did there.

The night we flew home from Calcutta to Delhi, we approached the tarmac for landing. It was very foggy, and we could hardly see any lights at the airport. It seemed like we were never going to touch down when suddenly the plane veered up sharply. I looked at Randy and said, "We're going back up again!" He confirmed that we were. We circled and approached the tarmac again, safely landing the second time. Once we safely landed, I asked my brother what he thought had happened.

Randy had a way of making people feel at ease and making them feel better about what was happening. I later realized that I looked to him to make me feel better about what had just happened. His answer to my question was that we either were short of the runway or had overshot the runway. There could have even been another airplane in our path. Then he said, "Don't worry, Sis, as long as I'm here, we're safe." I laughed and said, "Yeah, your eyes were bugging out of your head!" We both laughed nervously, never knowing what had happened or why. I had never flown that far from home or faced that kind of potential trauma. It was a true learning experience for me!

As we became better acquainted with one another and our separate families, my husband, Mike, and I would visit, trying to time our visits, so we could attend Randy's church and listen to him preach. We were invited to attend his 20th-year celebration of being the senior pastor of Griffin First Assembly of God. When we returned home that afternoon, he was ready to sit down and relax until the evening service. I told him that he couldn't sit down yet as he still had a job to do. I don't know what he expected, but when he looked at me, I told him that I wanted to accept Jesus into my heart as my Lord and Savior. It was a moment I will never forget, and when I embraced him, I know I felt a huge sigh of relief come from him.

Being born again is the best feeling, knowing that I can always lean on God, and I'm never alone. Not only did I find that having a new brother was a blessing to my life, but I also now had eternal life by accepting Christ as my Savior. I was later able to return to Griffin, where I was baptized in water by my brother.

|||||||||||||||||||||||||||||||||||||||||||||||||||||||||||||||||||||||||||||||||||||||

> Not only did I find that having a
> new brother was a blessing to my
> life, but I also now had eternal life
> by accepting Christ as my Savior.

Having a relationship with Jesus has brought a peace and calm to me.

JELLY'S THOUGHTS

Suzanne's most important conversation with Randy was not that she remembered his birth father or his birth. It was not the discovery of their genetic similarities. Although she provided answers to some of the questions that had plagued Randy for much of his life, the most important conversation came on the Sunday we celebrated twenty years in Griffin. Randy's favorite thing to do on Sunday afternoon was to sit in his big easy chair and relax to football, golf, baseball games on television, or occasionally, a John Wayne movie. He was getting ready to do that when Suzanne came into his office and informed him that he was not yet finished with his day.

As they walked into Randy's "man-cave," she explained to him that she needed prayer. She just didn't know that the coming conversation was an answer to Randy's prayer. From the moment he learned that he had birth siblings and birth parents that were still living, he began to pray for their salvation. He told me that although he could raise money for missions around the world, his most important mission was to win his own family, both adoptive and birth, to Christ. He was so very proud of his family—his ethnic roots—and he now wanted them to know Christ and to have the same opportunity to live for Christ.

When Randy met Suzanne, it was as if another puzzle piece of his heart, another thread of the tapestry, was woven into place. He loved his entire Valimont family so very much, but adding this first sister-of-the-heart made him feel as if this part of the journey, although filled with pain and heartache, had been so worth the effort. They became better and better acquainted with one another, family members, and their own little idiosyncrasies that no one would have ever imagined could possibly be genetic.

||||||||||||||||||||||||||||||||||||||||||||||||||||||||||||||||||||||||||||||||||||||

When Randy met Suzanne, it was as if another puzzle piece of his heart, another thread of the tapestry, was woven into place.

They spent hours talking and laughing on the telephone, as Randy mentored Suzanne in her new relationship with Jesus. Randy was both proud and humbled by the fact that he had a small part in bringing Suzanne to the true knowledge of who Jesus is and how much Jesus loves her. Randy watched her life change to include prayer, Bible study, and attending our church services online. Previously, none of this had been a part of her life, and Suzanne's daughter even commented on the changes she saw in her mom.

It seemed as if in the few short years of knowing one another, they made up for a lifetime of memories. It also gave Randy an added sense of destiny that he was able to share Christ with Suzanne and her family, and that she made a commitment to follow Christ. The day she made that commitment and the day of her baptism were deeply woven into this tapestry.

PARVIZ'S STORY

During the meeting with Marion, she openly told us about her affair with Parviz. At the time of Randy's conception, both Marion and Parviz were married but not to one another. Parviz had a wife and son in Iran, and Marion had a husband and four children in the same town. They were coworkers and frequently together in the workplace, so the relationship developed quickly and easily. Throughout the time they were together, Parviz met Marion's children and spent time with them, more so after Marion and her husband separated. Once Parviz was summoned back to Iran to perform surgery on the wife of the Shah, the affair was over, but Marion, unknowingly, carried a child.

When Parviz returned to the United States, he either learned that Marion was pregnant, too far along to abort the baby, or she never told him at all. She did state that he would never acknowledge the child as his own. We do not know if this is something Marion was told or assumed. It is a question that was never asked and never answered. She delivered Randy and immediately gave him up for adoption as neither her husband nor her lover wanted the child.

Once we were told this story, we understood Marion's dilemma. What a nightmare it would have been for Randy to be raised in a home where he was not wanted, in a town where he would see and know his birth father did not want him! There would have been no way to keep the circumstances of his birth a secret. To give him up for adoption was probably Marion's greatest sacrifice but also the best thing she could have done to ensure Randy would be raised in a loving and stable home where he could excel in life. Some might look at her act as one of selfishness, but once he knew the circumstances surrounding his conception, birth, and subsequent adoption, Randy was truly grateful.

After Marion gave this information to Randy, he wanted to make an initial call to his birth father, just to introduce himself. During the call, Parviz refused to acknowledge the affair, the pregnancy, or Randy's birth in any way. In fact, he stated that it was his brother who knew Marion; he did not. Randy, being the insistent person that he was, told Parviz that he wanted nothing from him but to hear his voice, and then Randy disconnected the call. Again, rejection. One of the interesting things to note about this conversation is that I noticed Randy and Parviz had the same voice quality. Although the accents were very different, they sounded very much alike on the telephone. When Randy ended the conversation, he exclaimed, "I sound just like him!"

It was the spring of 2003 when we discovered that we would be traveling to Boston, Massachusetts, for business. Brookline, the town where Parviz lived, was a suburb of Boston, and Randy wanted to have a face-to-face meeting with Parviz. It was not the best time in American history to travel to Boston to meet a man that we now knew was an Iranian Muslim. A lady who attended our church and worked in United States intelligence performed a security check on the family and found that we would be safe to contact Parviz. There were no flags or questions about his loyalty to the United States.

Once in Boston, Randy and I, along with two friends, traveled to the apartment where Parviz and his wife lived. Randy and Wayne sneaked into the lobby of the secured building while Sharon and I stood across the street, waiting to see what would happen. They told us to get ready to run if the building had security, and they needed to be bailed out of jail for unlawful entry!

When Parviz came to the door, he immediately recognized Randy. We assume that it was an obvious family resemblance, and he surmised Randy was the son he had rejected. He took one look at Randy and stated that he never wanted to see him, that he would never acknowledge him, and that he would never be a part of his life. Randy replied to Parviz, "I know you don't want to know me, but I wanted to see your face. I needed to know how you look and if I look like you. I also want you to know that Jesus loves you, and one day, you will need to know that." Parviz scoffed, turned, and walked away. It was never our intention to interfere or cause pain to Parviz or his family.

Upon our return to Georgia, at Randy's request, I wrote a letter to Parviz, introducing our family to him and telling him that we would never interfere in his life. I enclosed a family picture because I wanted him to see our family, to know that his birth son was a wonderful husband and father and was a successful man. We needed and wanted nothing from him. I also told him that this would be the only letter he would ever receive from us. There was no response, and we kept our promise to never initiate contact again. Should he have changed his mind and chosen to contact us, he now had the address and telephone numbers to do so.

Life settled into a new rhythm after adding four of Randy's maternal siblings into our family relationships, and we learned to navigate in a not-so-traditional family dynamic. Although we knew that Parviz had a son, Mohammed, and a daughter, Niloo, they were not a part of our lives. In fact, they did not know that Randy existed.

Our daughters knew Randy's story and were content to have both Randy's adoptive family and Marion's children as a part of our lives. However, as our girls grew, they had more questions that begged answers, especially about the mysterious Iranian side of the family. In fact, they all had a little identity crisis when they discovered that they were not of Italian descent but Iranian. Other than terrorist attacks, we had no perspective of the Iranian culture, no understanding of who or what might possibly be part of our future. What a joy it was to eventually be so honored to adopt part of the Iranian culture into ours!

Although I had made a commitment in my letter to Parviz and intended to keep my word, I kept my file filled with the information from the adoption websites where I registered, the private investigator's information, and all my notes about both sides of the family through the years. I also had pictures given to me by Marion and pictures I had taken from the internet. The file was not concise or thorough, but I wanted to keep the information should we ever again desire to reference it. There is a lot of information to find online when you are determined to have answers!

In 2015, Randy and I were traveling out of state when I received a call from Danielle. She had decided to do her own sleuthing and found that her dad had another birth brother and birth sister. She wanted to know if we knew, if we had pictures, if we had ever met them, where they lived, and if they knew about her dad. As I answered her questions to the best of my ability, she wanted to look at my notes to see if her sleuthing had been as good as mine or if I had information she did not have. She also has Randy's competitive gene! I told her where she could find and read my file; however, she was never to take it out of our home. She found it, read it, and I later found out that she did not take it but photocopied the entire file!

At the time, Danielle was working with Calcutta Mercy and was planning to conduct a volunteer training event in Boston, Massachusetts, in the following days. I did not know her ulterior motives for getting my file and doing more research about the family while she was in Boston. Later that week, I received a call from Danielle as she was sitting in the home of Randy's paternal birth brother, Mohammed.

||||||||||||||||||||||||||||||||||||||||||||||||||||||||||||||||||||||||||||||||||||||||||||||||

> Later that week, I received a call from Danielle as she was sitting in the home of Randy's paternal birth brother, Mohammed.

DANIELLE'S STORY

"Hi, I'm Danielle. I've spent the last seven years traveling the globe sharing stories of beautiful people for nonprofit organizations. I've been so moved being invited into their lives and have questioned why I've felt so at home among people I previously had never known. One thing I do know: Love transcends borders and cultures and oceans and religion and race and language like no one could ever fully explain, and maybe it's that love that's given me the courage to explore a story I haven't before—my own.

Today I drove to Weston, Massachusetts, to introduce myself to my father's brother. Unannounced. To give you a little context, my uncle didn't know he had a brother.

I imagined all the emotions they could feel: hurt that they didn't know, disbelief that I was who I said I was, and as my stomach tossed and turned, I played this conversation in my head. Emotions that I wasn't prepared for came up, and tears filled my eyes at the thought of the pain I might be causing them with their discovery of "us."

Suddenly this girl who had traveled the world alone, been fearless facing dark places, bungee jumped, and been in a plane that was emergency landed was scared.

Then I . . . I just did it. I rang the bell. And he answered.

My uncle. He answered the door.

My heart raced as I asked him his name. . . . Tears welled up in my eyes, and he invited me in and listened to me with the kindest and gentle, loving eyes you could imagine. His wife, my aunt, embraced me, and they rejoiced. Our family had just gotten bigger!

For hours, we shared all about each other's lives and families through pictures. Everyone agrees that Dad has the family eyebrows. We talked art and Iran (my heritage) and finished the evening over a Persian meal.

Before the night was over, I broke the news to my parents on a phone call. It went something like: 'So you won't believe what I did today. . . .' and ended with my father talking to his brother for the first time.

Some will say its coincidence that I arrived the night after my uncle's return from Germany . . . or ten minutes before he was to leave for a meeting . . . but I know the truth. Today, God made it happen."

JELLY'S THOUGHTS

After Danielle met Mohammed and tears from everyone were dried, Mohammed called and spoke to Randy for the first time. He was quite concerned that Randy had never contacted him and that Parviz had never acknowledged him. Niloo, Randy's sister, called shortly afterward and expressed the same concerns. Shortly thereafter, we met face-to-face in Atlanta. Again, genetics proved to have an extremely strong impact on birth siblings as Randy discovered so many likenesses between himself, his paternal birth siblings, and his nephews. In addition to previously understood knowledge about maternal genetic characteristics, Randy found that the paternal genetic, physical characteristics were extremely strong and repeated in him, his brother, and his nephews. Suddenly, he looked like someone else—almost exactly like someone else!

|||||||||||||||||||||||||||||||||||||||||||||||||||||||||||||||||||||||||||||||||||||||||

Suddenly, he looked like
someone else—almost exactly
like someone else!

One of the strongest physical characteristics was the eyebrows. The Fotouhi eyebrows. They are dominant in all the Fotouhi men and repeated generation after generation. That is probably the first thing we noticed about the men in Randy's paternal family. If any physical thing connected them, it was the eyebrows!

MOHAMMED AND NILOO'S STORY

It was Sunday, June 13, 2015. My wife, Parvine, and I were getting ready to go out when the doorbell rang. When I opened the door, an attractive young lady was standing there. "Can I help you with something?" I asked. She replied with another question, "Are you Mohammed Fotouhi?" Puzzled, I hesitantly said yes. What came next changed our lives forever: "My father is your brother."

I was stunned, shocked, and confused. Parvine asked the emotional young lady into the house and guided her to our study, where she introduced herself as Danielle Valimont, the middle daughter of Randy Valimont, a pastor in Griffin, Georgia. Once we had regained our composure, we asked Danielle to come back a bit later in the afternoon since we had a prior commitment elsewhere.

When we returned and pulled into the driveway to our house, Danielle was already there waiting for us. Danielle explained that around 2002, her father, Randy, had begun a search for his biological parents. He had discovered that his biological father, Dr. Parviz Fotouhi, was alive and residing in Brookline, Massachusetts. Shortly after, Randy had reached out to our father and tried to visit him, but unfortunately, our father was not receptive. He had sent him a Persian/Farsi Bible but had never tried to contact him or anyone in my family. Danielle said that in 2015, she came across the investigator's report in her mother's files and discovered that her father had a brother in Weston, Massachusetts. During a business trip to Boston on that fateful Sunday, she decided to look up her uncle.

Parvine, Danielle, and I had a lovely dinner at a Persian restaurant, and I talked on the telephone with my younger brother for the first time. It was a very emotional time. On the one hand, I was happy to learn that I had a brother, and on the other hand, I was forced to come to terms with my father's actions. He had either not believed Randy when he tried to visit with him, or he had believed Randy, who was ten years my junior, and had decided to protect my mother, my sister, and me. At the time that Danielle visited us, our mother had already passed away, but my sister, Niloo, and I are certain that she would have welcomed Randy into our family with open arms.

After our visit with Danielle, I called Niloo, who lives in Arizona with her family, with the incredible news. Niloo was thrilled and overjoyed. I remember her excitement during our telephone conversation. Her only question to me was, "How soon can we fly to Georgia to meet Randy?" Without hesitation, we decided on the upcoming July 4 weekend. Parvine and I flew from Boston, while Niloo and her son, Eric, flew from Scottsdale, Arizona, so we could meet our brother and his family. Meanwhile, our father was dividing his time between Boston and Scottsdale after our mother had passed away. Since he was recovering from a complicated surgery after the removal of a malignant tumor in his pancreas, we decided not to share our news with him at that time.

The Fotouhi family, and by extension Randy, is from the Azerbaijan region in the western part of Iran. Our heritage dates to the Qajar dynasty. Our great-grandfather, Fotouh-al-Molk Mohammed Fotouhi, was a landed elite in Azerbaijan. He was bestowed fifteen farming villages by the Qajar monarch for his loyalty and accomplishments during the Qajar reign. Fotouh-al-Molk had three sons and one daughter. Each of his children inherited a number of those villages, including our branch of the family, headed by Farid Issa Fotouhi, known as Haji Farid. Our grandfather, Issa, had nine children. Randy, my sister, and I have thirty-five cousins! Some have passed away. I am the oldest male grandchild of the Fotouhi clan, and now I am the oldest living patriarch of the family.

The family wealth was redistributed by decree of the Shah Mohammad Reza Pahlavi (monarch of Iran from 1941 to 1979) during the White Revolution in the early 1960s. At the height of the Cold War between the United States and the Soviet Union, thwarting the spread of communism became the policy of democratic governments around the globe. The United States during the Kennedy administration was no exception. Iran, at that time, was the most important US ally in the Middle East. During the Kennedy administration, foreign policy-makers believed that certain reforms within Iran would prevent a communist-style revolution, as well as a possible overthrow of the Shah. One of these reforms was aimed at the landed elite.

Under orders from the Kennedy administration, the Shah directed his government to pay the landed elite a token sum for their farmland, equivalent to a few cents per hectare, and to proceed with the reallocation of these lands to farmers. Prized agricultural property, including ours, was either "gifted" to the government or forcibly taken and distributed to the villagers across the country. Property owners were allowed to keep their homes and small orchards. In retrospect, the White Revolution failed: rural economies were adversely altered, and agricultural farmers and workers were forced to migrate to big cities in search of jobs and better wages.

Issa Fotouhi gifted his land to the government, losing the bulk of his estate. Among his nine children, only one son benefitted from the sale of a portion of the land using his full power of attorney, which he had garnered from all his siblings and our father—Parviz. Unfortunately, the proceeds were not distributed as intended, and our father and his siblings did not receive their fair share of the family inheritance. However, this was not the defining moment for Issa's children. Over half a century later, our lives truly changed forever when we met Randy and his family for the first time at Rumi's Kitchen in Atlanta.

|||||||||||||||||||||||||||||||||||||||||||||||||||||||||||||||||||||||||||||||||||||||

> Our lives truly changed forever
> when we met Randy and his
> family for the first time.

I recall Niloo walking into the restaurant and just stopping when she saw Randy. She looked at him, then at me, and then at him again. She said, "He looks exactly like Papa!" and then rushed to hug him. We met Jelly, Jordan, Alayna, Jaeli, and of course, Danielle, who was instrumental in bringing us together. On the same weekend, Randy took us all to visit the Coca-Cola headquarters—obviously a big hit with Eric and Jaeli! On Sunday, we visited Randy's church, First Assembly of God, in Griffin, Georgia, and attended the service. Parvine, Niloo, Eric, and I felt so welcome.

After the service, we had lunch together, and we learned about each other. We were amazed at Randy's accomplishments, the childhood adversities he had to overcome, and the man that he was. He was a loving husband, an amazing father, a doting grandfather, and an inspirational leader.

When Niloo returned home, she talked to our father about Randy. He was not convinced and believed it to be impossible. Our father had originally left Iran to pursue his medical residency and fellowship in upstate New York around 1952, when I was two years old. I did not see our father again until 1959 when my mother and I joined him in the United States. We lived in Oneonta, New York, on the grounds of what was then known as the Homer Folks Hospital until 1960, when my dad completed his work. Dwight D. Eisenhower was president, and we flew back on one of the first modern passenger jet airplanes.

Niloo was born in 1964. I recall Randy telling me that when he found his biological mother and connected with her, she told him that my dad did not know he had a son in America. Niloo and I were not surprised by our father's reaction when Randy visited my dad in 2003 for the first time. It must have been a huge shock to meet Randy. My dad was not aware that he had another son. Randy was put up for adoption at birth, and to the best of our knowledge, Randy's mother had never contacted our father.

A short time after our visit with Randy, I went to Scottsdale on business. This was the best opportunity for Niloo and me to speak with our father again. Our father understood how important this was to all of us—that he could meet his son, his daughter-in-law, his grandchildren, and his great-granddaughter. We settled on the Fotouhi family reunion, which had been planned for December 2015 in Laguna Beach, California. Papa and Randy could meet, and we could officially introduce Randy and the Valimonts to all the Fotouhis.

Subject: Mohammed & Niloo share some very exciting news!

Dear Family,

Mohammed and I would like to take this opportunity to share very happy and exciting news with you all.

We recently found out that we have a brother!

When our dad, Parviz, was geographically and emotionally separated from our mother for 8-9 years while pursuing his medical studies in the US, he formed a mutually affectionate relationship with someone. After he had returned to Iran, his companion realized that she was pregnant and chose to give up this child for adoption. Fast-forward many years, our brother, Randy Valimont, searched for his family and found his birth mother. Through his biological mother, he was able to find us!

He is married to a wonderful lady, Jelly, and has three lovely daughters, Jordan, Danielle, and Alayna and one grand-daughter, Jaeli. Thanks to Danielle's persistence, we have been united with Randy.

We know that you will welcome them into the family when you meet them next week—as only Fotouhis can do! Actually, Randy and his family are Fotouhis!

Much love,

Niloo & Mohammed

Unfortunately, a few weeks before the reunion, our father had a relapse, and the prognosis was not good. Nevertheless, he insisted that we move forward with the planned festivities. The reunion was a great success. My cousins embraced Randy, Jelly, Danielle, Alayna, and Jaeli. I watched with amazement and pride—Randy had won them over with his charm and grace.

After the reunion, Randy, my cousin Rebecca Lambert, my son, Nader, Niloo, Eric, and I took a flight back to Phoenix and went directly to see our father. Randy and my dad were finally together. Even though our father was very frail, he was alert, excited, and proud to meet Randy. You could see the joy in his face.

Nader and I flew back to California to meet Parvine and his sisters, Leila and Rana. Randy and Rebecca stayed another day with Niloo to visit with our father. Sadly, our father's condition worsened shortly after this meeting. Niloo spent the rest of the week by his side at hospice. She called us on January 4, 2016, when my dad passed away—only a few days after meeting Randy. Niloo and I are certain that they both had closure, and we are grateful to have played a small role in that. We are both very much at peace.

Niloo and I, along with our families, were very fortunate to spend time with Randy and his family over the next two years. Randy and Jelly joined us for a private celebration of our father in Boston, on what would have been his 95th birthday.

We met Randy and the Valimonts again later that summer at Pebble Beach for a Fire Bible event, where we had the pleasure of meeting some of Randy's closest friends, as well as members of his congregation. My son, Nader, and Randy bonded during that weekend. Both are avid golfers. When I look back, I fondly remember how it seemed to me as if Randy and Nader had known each other all their lives—not just for a mere few months. Randy had a similar relationship with my nephew, Eric, who adored him.

On other occasions, Randy visited with Niloo when vacationing in Arizona, and we were all together again for Danielle's wedding to

Praveen in Georgia in August 2019. Regardless of where he was or what he was doing, Randy would always keep in touch. He often sent texts or called Niloo just to say, "I was thinking of you. I love you li'l sis." He would call me, and we would chat about anything and everything.

A few days before his surgery, Randy called Niloo and me separately. I was in New York City on a business trip, and Niloo was in Phoenix. It was a Friday. Niloo and I have the same recollection of our individual conversations with Randy. I remember I was walking on Lexington Avenue on my way to a meeting. Randy always called me "my brother." He said, "My brother, I am going for elective surgery on Tuesday, and I wanted to make sure you knew in case you heard it from someone else." I asked him about his procedure and told him that I was well connected to the medical community in the Boston area—I wanted him in Boston for the procedure. He said that he preferred to be in Griffin where he felt at home, knew the people in the hospital, and would be well taken care of. I told him that I would come to Atlanta on the day after his surgery to see him. I think he was happy to hear that.

The day after Randy's surgery, I traveled to Atlanta and saw him in his hospital room. He appeared to be in good spirits, and Jelly was taking excellent care of him. I was pleased to see Jordan and Jaeli, who were there to see "Papa." Randy and I walked twice in the hallways of the hospital as we chatted. I left Atlanta that night thinking that he was in excellent hands and in good spirits. I was happy to see him recovering. Niloo was also in constant contact with Randy. When she couldn't talk to Randy, she was texting or calling Jelly or the girls.

A few days after the original surgery, Randy required a follow-up procedure. Due to unforeseen complications, he did not recover from the second surgery. Randy had passed. Niloo and I were devastated, as were Parvine, Nader, and Eric. In a span of three short years, we had found our brother, and we had lost him. Randy left a great impression on our lives. His faith, his positivity, and his joy for life were inspirational. We will miss him, always.

JELLY'S THOUGHTS

One of the many things that amazed me about Mohammed and Niloo was their readiness to accept Randy as their brother. There was no apparent shame or confusion as to how this could have happened with their father. In fact, from the beginning of the first conversation, Mohammed said to Randy, "My brother, why have I not known about you all of your life?" In turn, Niloo told Randy, "I have always wanted another brother."

||||||||||||||||||||||||||||||||||||||||||||||||||||||||||||||||||||||||||||||||||||

> Mohammed said to Randy, "My brother, why have I not known about you all of your life?" In turn, Niloo told Randy, "I have always wanted another brother."

At the time, I did not realize that this acceptance was a part of their family culture. Randy's paternal grandfather, a Muslim, had a wife and a concubine, their unions resulting in ten children who all lived on the same estate with both mothers equally caring for the children. Parviz was one of the ten, and in their minds, should have been readily accepting of a child resulting from an affair. The extended family did not understand why he would not accept Randy. I can only surmise that there was something greater at stake that no one understood. Had Parviz accepted Randy as his son, Randy would probably not have been raised in a Christian home and not have had the opportunity to follow God's call into ministry.

Within a few short weeks, Mohammed and Niloo informed their father that they had met Randy and his family. Parviz was very ill and expressed regret for not allowing Randy to be a part of their lives. However, Parviz was able to initially meet the Valimont family through pictures and conversation. A family reunion was planned and underway for December 2015. The entire extended family would plan to meet our family. They would come from France, Iran, Thailand, England, and all over the United States. We would come from Georgia to meet the Iranian family and begin relationships with the paternal side of the family.

From this meeting, multiple threads would be woven into the tapestry of Randy's life, bringing more clarity to the picture that God was weaving.

Much to our dismay, Parviz became very ill during the months preceding the reunion. He had a recurrence of cancer and would be unable to attend the reunion due to his failing health. After the reunion, Randy traveled to Scottsdale, Arizona, where Parviz was living his last few days on earth. I left California to return home with the family, intending to travel to Arizona the following week. Once Randy was in Arizona, Parviz expressed his regret and sorrow for his actions toward Randy as Niloo recorded the conversation.

They were able to sit and converse for about an hour before Randy had to leave for home. During that emotional meeting, Parviz said some of the most important things to Randy that every man—every adoptee—needs to hear:

1) I am sorry; please forgive me.
2) I love you.
3) I am proud of you.

Throughout his life, Randy had lived never knowing if his birth parents would have been proud of who he had become. He did not know if they would have cared that he was successful and loved. In that one meeting while Parviz was on his deathbed, he answered the cry of Randy's heart, answered the unspoken questions. Randy left the meeting never knowing if he would see his birth father again but knowing that he finally had the acceptance for which he had longed.

We do not know if Parviz made a commitment to follow the teachings of Jesus, but we do know that many prayers were said that he would have an encounter with Jesus before his death. Parviz died a few days later before the rest of our family and I could travel to Arizona to meet him.

CHAPTER 7

ACCEPTANCE

Forgiving those who provided
the threads for the tapestry

Relationships are important to all of us. Throughout life, many relationships are begun and ended. Some are forged in fire while others are seemingly irreparably broken. Hurt and pain occur in all families. Even through brokenness and rejection, the grace and goodness of God can bring restoration.

We often do not understand why relationships end or what we could have done to change the outcome of the relationship. What we fail to take into consideration is that these relationships are just threads that must be woven into the tapestry of our lives. Some of those threads are there to stay and provide an entire part of the picture, but others are just small threads that only provide a measure of dimension to our tapestry. The brokenness and rejection of a relationship are only a part of the tapestry—not the whole—unless we choose to make it the entire tapestry. It is our choice. Everyone has to choose what to do with circumstances that occur. We can take the circumstances, the brokenness, and the rejection and weave our entire lives around their pain, or we can allow God to make it only a moment—a portion—of our lives that He can use.

||||||||||||||||||||||||||||||||||||||||||||||||||||||||||||||||||||||||||||||||||||||||||

We can take the circumstances, the brokenness, and the rejection and weave our entire lives around their pain, or we can allow God to make it only a moment—a portion—of our lives that He can use.

Randy never had the opportunity to develop a close relationship with either Parviz or Marion. He DID have the opportunity to know the initial betrayal of their marriage vows and of himself at his birth. They provided life, but they had only a small part at the beginning. They were a part of his tapestry but did not provide his entire life plan. There came a point in Randy's life when he had to recognize that although his tapestry was begun by Marion and Parviz, he needed to forgive them to move on and fulfill the destiny of God in his life. That destiny could only come through forgiveness—not anger and bitterness. It was a choice that he made to forgive.

The decision to forgive was pivotal in determining his destiny. You see, one cannot be angry and bitter, and at the same time, believe God to bring restoration, a future, and blessing. Randy wanted to be a man of peace, to live in forgiveness and blessing. He had needed answers which he found, but the question he now faced was what he would do with those answers. Psalm 37:37 (ESV) says, "Mark the blameless and behold the upright, for there is a future for the man of peace." Randy wanted to be blameless and not hold close the rejection he had felt most of his life. He wanted to live and walk in forgiveness and have a future of peace. To do that, he had to truly forgive.

One of the things to note about forgiveness is that it is an act that is born out of a need. To forgive someone means that there is a need to forgive someone! Randy knew he needed to forgive, but he also knew that there might never be an opportunity to restore or bring about a close relationship with either of his birth parents. He knew that he might need to ask God daily to help him forgive the feelings of rejection he had felt most of his life. However, just because he experienced the act of forgiveness did not necessarily bring him to a place of restoration. Forgiveness is an act; restoration is a place. Some things may never be restored, and we have to learn to be okay with that as long as there is no unforgiveness in our hearts.

In Genesis 37:18-28, we read part of the story of Joseph. He was a favored son of Jacob (the Deceiver) and Rachel. Joseph was also known as the Dreamer. He had dreams and visions that were directly from God, and his telling of those dreams to his family often got him into trouble with them! As a result of his favored status and his dreams, the sibling rivalry became unmanageable and his brothers placed him into a pit, possibly planning to leave him there indefinitely. His brother Reuben intended to return to the pit and rescue him, but Reuben was too late. Joseph had been sold into slavery, and another portion of the tapestry for Joseph had been put into action.

Joseph was probably beaten repeatedly by his captors, enduring great suffering and shame. His ability to withstand the beatings and shame would have made him a more valuable commodity, and he would have commanded a higher price. Prisoners easily and quickly lost their dignity. However, Joseph had a dream from God, and it was that dream that took him through the difficulty. Joseph's dream first took him to the pit, but ultimately it took him through the pit.

When you awake in difficulty and find yourself a slave or a prisoner because of the machinations of someone else, don't give up on the dream that God has given you. God is not yet finished. The plan of God is at work. The hurt may be deep. The circumstances may be insurmountable, but God is at work. He is still weaving a tapestry, and it is not yet finished.

> When you awake in difficulty and find yourself a slave or a prisoner because of the machinations of someone else, don't give up on the dream that God has given you.

As far as rights are concerned, in this story of Joseph, we find that he had every right to be bitter. His own family had sold him into bondage and betrayed the family relationship. Potiphar's wife had lied and accused him of assault. He was immediately found guilty because he was a slave, a servant in bondage. After serving a significant amount of time in prison for the alleged assault, Joseph's friend, who had promised to intercede for him, forgot to mention Joseph to the authorities, so he could be set free. Joseph interpreted dreams with no remuneration and languished in prison for thirteen years. It was not fair, especially as Joseph had done nothing wrong; however, in this time of bondage, God wanted to teach Joseph how to depend on Him. God would eventually bring Joseph to a place of restoration and salvation for his own family. It was not immediate, and Joseph's tapestry was just being woven; it wasn't completed. Joseph had no idea of how God was going to weave a picture of forgiveness, restoration, and rescue through him for his family.

All restoration begins with forgiveness, not bitterness. When Joseph saw his family for the first time in many years, he had somehow already released the anger and bitterness that could have dwelled in his heart. He somehow put himself into a position so that God could use him to help his family and begin the process of restoration.

Something happened in Joseph's heart between the time he was sold into the hands of the Midianites and the time he went into Potiphar's house. He did not nurture bitterness and turn away from God. It was Joseph's choice that bitterness would not become his bondage. As he CHOSE to walk the path of forgiveness and restoration, Joseph began to excel in his place of betrayal, his school of slavery, because he did not allow it to dictate the remainder of his life. He did not stay in slavery to the rejection from his family. He did not remain in the bitterness he could have nourished. Joseph decided that he would survive or die. As a result, God blessed all that Joseph touched, and Joseph was elevated to a place of honor and leadership over the country of Egypt. If we can learn anything from the life of Joseph, we should learn that our circumstances do not have to result in slavery to the circumstance.

||||||||||||||||||||||||||||||||||||||||||||||||||||||||||||||||||||||||||||||||||

> If we can learn anything from
> the life of Joseph, we should
> learn that our circumstances
> do not have to result in slavery
> to the circumstance.

In one day, through supernatural events and the interpretation of dreams, God took Joseph from the prison of slavery into the palace of the king. Had Joseph not lived a life of forgiveness, he could not have been placed before the king. God cannot bless bitterness, but He can bless truth. Truth and forgiveness can make you free. It can change your life and restore your relationships, giving you a God-perspective on your brokenness.

Can we forgive and resist the temptation to become bitter when we have been wronged? During our difficulty, we have an opportunity to resist the spirit of offense. You may feel that you have a right to your anger and frustration. Can you forget betrayal and brokenness? Will you bury yourself in bitterness and bondage or ask the Lord for wisdom and grace? Joseph made a declaration by willfully forgetting. Joseph named his son Manasseh which means, "God has made me forget entirely my troubles and my father's house." Did Joseph really forget? Was it wiped from his mind? He did not actually forget his father and his brothers; however, when he remembered his father's house and the years of his youth, the memory had no ability to dredge up feelings of hurt, heartache, and pain. He remembered his father and his brothers but did not hold to their account the wrongs committed against him.

Whenever Joseph spoke the name of his son Ephraim, meaning "God has blessed me," he declared that he was willing to forget the toil, the heartache, and the pain of brokenness and remember the goodness of blessings. God had made Joseph forget the hardship and the pain of the past, and Joseph made a choice to not continue to remember. It was a willful act, a declaration of Joseph's forgiveness of those who had wronged him.

Sometimes we choose to remember the heartbreak and brokenness of the past. We revisit the moment when we realize that we have been betrayed, that someone has caused us or those we love immeasurable pain. We remember our failures and are sure it is God reminding us of how we have messed up the plan He has for our lives. We play the movie in our heads repeatedly, wanting a different outcome at the end of the movie but knowing that the end will remain the same. We allow ourselves to remember the pain, and we refuse to put it in a place where God can help us forgive. That pain then turns into anger and bitterness when it is unresolved. The anger and bitterness then thwart our faith in God and in His ability to help us walk into His purpose for our lives. Faith cannot fight with bitterness and unforgiveness attached to our sides, being our constant companions. By remembering and dwelling on past pain, we cannot move forward into our destiny.

There are things that happen in our lives that we need to intentionally and willfully forget. It was only after Joseph intentionally and willfully forgot the pain of His past life that he recognized the blessings and favor of God in his life. You may have been through heartache, but if you choose, God can *Manasseh* "make you forget your troubles," and you will recognize that God *Ephraim* "has blessed you." Just because difficulty comes into our lives does not mean that God will stop using the gifts in our lives. It just means that we may have to discover different or more purposeful ways to use those gifts.

When our youngest daughter, Alayna, was born prematurely, the doctors told us that she would possibly be blind, deaf, have lung and breathing issues, learning disabilities, and would struggle physically throughout her life. We had tentatively named her "Abigail," meaning "her father's joy," but we changed her name to "Alayna Nicole," meaning "Princess of victory." Every time we said her name, it was a declaration of our faith that God's promise would be fulfilled, and He would bring victory. We chose to not just believe she would bring joy but that even her name would be a statement of faith and trust in God. We can point back to the time when we decided that regardless of what might come, we were going to live for Jesus and believe His Word. She lives today, completely healthy and whole, with no learning disabilities or physical issues. She IS truly a princess of victory.

It was only after Randy met his birth parents and made a conscious decision to forgive them for giving him away and for rejecting him that healing began to come into his heart. He recognized the divine appointment from God for his life and began to see the blessings of being given up for adoption. He had already chosen not to live with anger and bitterness, but his heartache still had the ability to cause him the immense pain of rejection. Healing came through truly letting go of the past and allowing God to continue to weave the threads of his life into a tapestry that was worthy of a master weaver. He began to understand that this was all part of the ultimate tapestry that God was weaving. Although there were hurtful circumstances and painful memories, God still had a purpose and a plan that He was weaving and fulfilling.

||||||||||||||||||||||||||||||||||||||||||||||||||||||||||||||||||||||||||||||||||

Healing came through truly letting go of the past and allowing God to continue to weave the threads of his life into a tapestry that was worthy of a master weaver.

CHAPTER 8

DESTINY

Seeing the Predrawn Plan

Who am I? Where did I come from? What am I doing? What am I supposed to do? Where am I going? Is there something more for me? Why did God make me? Who did He design me to be? Is God even real? Does He care about me? What do I do next? Have I screwed up my life so badly that I can't recover, be used by God, or influence anyone for the greater good? When will I ever understand what I am going through? Am I truly enduring? Is there a purpose for my pain? All of these are legitimate questions, probably asked by many throughout history.

While we may one day have some of the answers, we may never see the full picture, the beautiful tapestry that God is designing; however, we CAN rest assured that God has a plan, a purpose, a destiny for us. He wants to use our lives, our stories, to make an impact for eternity. Not just today and tomorrow: ETERNITY. How does it feel knowing that God can and will use you to impact others forever, that you can do something good with your life that will never be forgotten by God?

Psalm 57:2 (ESV, emphasis added) says,

> *"I cry out to* **God** *Most High, to* **God** *who*
> *fulfills his* **purpose for me.** *"*

We all make decisions in life that can determine our destiny. We may mistakenly think that our purpose is our destiny, and although they are tied together, they are two separate things. Often people will miss the divine plan and the purpose that God has placed before them because they are not looking for it or do not recognize it as being part of the plan of God for their lives. Another reason we can miss the divine plan is because we focus on the pain of the past, the brokenness, and the hardships we have endured. We complain about the negative things that have happened rather than spend time focusing on the blessings we have encountered. Our attitudes affect what God can do in us and may eventually thwart our destiny.

If we want to be all that God has designed us to be, to fulfill His purpose in us and our destinies, we must learn to develop a sensitivity to the things of God by spending time with Him and learning to hear, truly hear, His voice. I am personally convinced that if a person wants to hear, know, and understand God, if they want to be all that God has designed them to be, if they want to do well in their journey, they develop an understanding of their season and put the hardships in the past.

We may think that what we are doing right now is fulfilling our destiny, but it may be a temporary purpose or a task and not the entire tapestry. This is part of developing an understanding of the season of your life or part of the picture in your tapestry. This does not last forever. It is only a part of the whole. In addition, you may never fully understand the reason for this part of your life, your tapestry depicting the season in which you may be living. The purpose of this time in your life is to set the stage for your destiny to be fulfilled.

According to The People Experience[5], purpose may be the reason something is done or created or the reason something exists. Our purpose gives us something to live for, something to look toward, and may even drive us to do the next important thing in our lives. Purpose matters, just as our day-to-day choices and actions matter, but destiny is the result of purpose!

||||||||||||||||||||||||||||||||||||||||||||||||||||||||||||||||||||||||||||||||||

> ## Purpose matters, just as our day-to-day choices and actions matter, but destiny is the result of purpose!

Let me give you a simple example: As I am writing this book, I am also renovating my home to move my mother, who is a widow in her later years, in with me. She is still independent, drives, goes to her own church, cooks, and shops. She does her own thing. However, the time has come for her to break up housekeeping and not be concerned about paying bills, grocery shopping, and overseeing the maintenance of her own home. There is a process for and a purpose in doing this. It must all be planned and done in order so that the transition will go as smoothly as possible for her.

---

5 Klaer Brooker, "Purpose: The Reason for Which Something Exists or Is Done, Made and Used; to Set as an Aim, Intention, or Goal," The People Experience, 19 Feb. 2018, http://thepeopleexperience.com/purpose-reason-something-exists-done-made-used-set-aim-intention-goal/.

Yes, the process is messy, detailed, and somewhat confusing, but the purpose is so the remaining years she has will be simple and filled with family, laughter, and joy. Her destiny has not always been to move in with me but to raise a Godly family who carries the gospel to the world. Today, her children and their spouses are serving the Lord. Her children were all in ministry, and seven of her grandchildren are in either full-time or marketplace ministry. Is her destiny being fulfilled? Yes, but I think her tapestry is still being woven!

We all have a purpose, a journey, so to speak, and a goal that has been set for us. When the tapestry of our lives is being woven, there are certain places in the picture where we begin to see what God has appointed us to do—our purpose. That purpose may change as the picture emerges and as the journey progresses. That does not mean that our destiny has changed! We are still headed toward the completed picture, the pre-drawn plan.

"The Lord will fulfill his purpose for me; your steadfast love, O Lord, endures forever. Do not forsake the work of your hands."
—Psalm 138:8 (ESV)

"I will cry to God Most High, Who performs on my behalf and rewards me [Who brings to pass His purposes for me and surely completes them]!"
—Psalm 57:2 (AMP)

This is one example of how Randy's purpose changed: When Randy was a young man, he desired to earn a degree in business. He knew he would be equipped to do business because he was already good at managing the business where he was currently employed. It was one of his many gifts. He went to college to study business, and although he did not complete the degree, he did learn some amazing principles for developing and facilitating a business.

His purpose for that time was to learn the semantics of business. It was only when he truly answered the call of God to go into full-time ministry that his purpose changed. He was no longer pursuing business, but he was pursuing ministry. After Randy walked into ministry, the business practices that he learned were invaluable, as he used them to fulfill the destiny of God on his life in ministry. He was prepared to help various ministries facilitate business plans, raise money in capital fundraising, and maintain a multimillion-dollar ministry in the church where he was the lead pastor. He had a purpose, but that purpose was not his destiny. His passions and his gifts met with his purpose to be woven into his destiny. God did not take him out of his giftings for the sole purpose of doing ministry, but God did take him out of his comfort zone! I believe the reason for this was, as it is for all of us, to develop his gifts and his character.

||||||||||||||||||||||||||||||||||||||||||||||||||||||||||||||||||||||||||||||||||||

God did not take Randy out of his giftings for the sole purpose of doing ministry, but God did take him out of his comfort zone!

Randy recognized some of the God-gifts early in his life, but he had no idea of his destiny that was yet to unfold. Randy always felt the destiny of God was strong on his life, and yet he wanted to do more. He wanted to see his destiny fulfilled and have clarity on exactly what God was doing. However, God's plans are rarely revealed in their entirety. They are more often revealed one step at a time. Randy, like all of us, was specifically set aside for a specific plan, one purpose, one step, one thread at a time.

God has a destiny for each of us. Our destiny will be determined by our decisions, our obedience, our faith, and our trust. Where you are right now may be different from where you want to be or where God wants you to ultimately fulfill what He has called you to do. Your destiny is whatever your appointed or ordained future may be, and God will fulfill it in you.

You have a purpose and a destiny that have been set before you. Although they are related, your purpose is tied to the season of your life right now. Your destiny does not change. To phrase it differently, your purpose may be based on the next right thing that you are supposed to do. The next open door that you walk through is part of your purpose; however, your destiny is still tied to the final picture that God is ultimately weaving in your tapestry. Many threads—many parts of the picture—must be placed in the loom for it to be accomplished. The completed picture, the tapestry has not changed. It is not over until God says it is over. Don't give up on the destiny that He has for your life.

We may look at our lives and see the picture, the tapestry, and be sure that there is more to be added before the product is finished. It doesn't seem that the story has been completely told. Then there are times when we look at the span of our lives and ask ourselves, *How much more can possibly be added?* or, *What else can happen?* I have always believed in the sovereignty of God and know that He—the Master Weaver—is ultimately in charge. There is no satanic attack, no demon or devil that will ever be victorious over Christ. In fact, everything that happens to me or mine must first be "Father-filtered." Everything first goes through my heavenly Father to get to me.

Human frailty, satanic attacks, and our mistakes may sometimes seem to thwart God's plans. There are things that happen that we do not understand, strings of the tapestry that are added that seem to not belong in that place, at that time. Things happen that totally take us by surprise. However, I know that nothing takes God by surprise. He is omnipotent (all-powerful), omniscient (all-knowing), and omnipresent (always present). God does not look down from heaven in shock and ask, "What will I do with this mistake My child just made?" Nothing puzzles or confuses Him. He sees the tapestry at its beginning, during the years of weaving and tamping down, and at its completion.

||||||||||||||||||||||||||||||||||||||||||||||||||||||||||||||||||||||||||||||||||||

Nothing takes God by surprise.

Throughout the Word of God, we see men and women of destiny who were adopted and grew to adulthood outside of their natural, biological families. They were people who knew that God had a predetermined plan for them to follow and a bigger, better plan than they could ever put in place themselves, even if they did not know how that plan would unfold, what would be their next purpose, or what tapestry God was weaving into their lives.

From the moment Moses was born and adopted into Pharaoh's household, God had a plan (Exodus 2). It was only after Moses spent years on the back side of a desert and saw a burning bush that was not consumed by the fire that Moses began to see part of God's plan unfold. As a result of this moment in time, Moses was responsible for saving the entire nation of Israel.

After the death of her parents, Esther was adopted into the home of her uncle and then taken into the king's home to become a part of his household. She became a favored queen and was put into that place for the specific purpose of saving her people. When a plan was put into action to destroy her people, she was in a place to help save them. Her uncle, who had raised her, told her that she had been placed there and that the destiny of God was on her life, "For such a time as this" (Esther 4:14).

As a young child, Samuel was given to the house of Eli the prophet so that he could be raised to be one of God's servants. His barren mother made a promise to God that if He would give her a child, she would give him back to God. Part of Samuel's destiny was to establish the monarchy of the nation of Israel and to bring righteousness back into the kingdom (1 and 2 Samuel).

Jesus was adopted by Joseph when Mary found that she was pregnant with the Son of God (Matthew 1:17-19). His destiny as a God-man was to bring salvation to the entire human race.

God's plan of destiny affected the lives of these people, but of all of these examples, only Jesus truly understood the destiny that God had placed on his life. Although we may have a sense of God's destiny for us, we may never fully understand or define it. BUT the fact that we may not know does not change the fact that God always has a plan, a purpose, and a destiny.

Our heavenly Father knows the picture that is being woven before it is ever begun and certainly before it is finished. He is the only One who sees the past, present, and future at the same time. The entire tapestry image is always entirely visible to Him. He not only sees us as we were in the past, but He sees us as we are now and how we will be in the future. He designs the tapestry knowing how it will appear at the end. What we think may be unfinished and illogical makes perfect sense to the Master Weaver because He sees it all.

I cannot tell you when it began to happen, but at some time, we began to see the tapestry of Randy's life (and mine) become a visible picture. The threads that God had begun to weave so many years before were becoming beautiful in His design. We may have noticed it when Randy began to travel and speak. It could have been at the altars during our church services as Randy ministered one-on-one to so many different people who were hurting, feeling betrayed, neglected, or rejected. It could have been when he was talking on the telephone, encouraging those he mentored, and expressing his pride in them and all they were accomplishing. It could have been when he ministered to the waiter or the waitress before they took our food order, as he asked how he could pray with them that day. I really don't know.

I cannot tell you when it began to happen, but at some time, we began to see the tapestry of Randy's life (and mine) become a visible picture.

What I do know is that a picture began to come into focus, and we began to see it somewhat more clearly. I can remember as we reflected on what God was doing in our lives, Randy once exclaimed to me, "This is what I was born to do!" He had begun to see and marvel at the work of God in his life and in the lives of others.

Randy faced his feelings of inadequacy and allowed God to begin to refine those feelings so that he could become what God ultimately wanted him to become, not what he alone thought he should be. Although he wanted to be accepted and affirmed, he knew that the inadequacy and ineptitude that sprung from deep in his psyche were only feelings and not facts. His most important life goal was to be pleasing to His heavenly Father and to become all he needed to be for the kingdom. He knew that although people looked at the size of the church and the enormity of what God was doing in the ministries of the church, the glory belonged to God, not to him. If he did not take credit for what God was doing, God would continue to bless.

There is a scripture—1 Corinthians 13:12 (KJV)—that says, *"For now we see through a glass darkly; but then face to face. . . ."*

This scripture is specifically referring to seeing clearly after eternity begins. Sometimes, we get an early glimpse of what God is doing in our lives. At other times, we don't see, don't understand, or cannot get clarity on life, and then a moment of epiphany will occur. When it occurs, we may exclaim, "Oh, that is why this happened!"

In Randy's life, we did not have one specific moment but many moments when God revealed part of His plan. There were also times when we did not understand where His hand was leading us but found that it was necessary for us to learn to listen for and trust His voice. That is how we knew that one day, we as a couple and as individuals would fulfill our destiny: by following the will of God for our lives.

If Randy had spent his entire life in bitterness, complaining about the fact that he was rejected, given away, and adopted, he would have missed the blessings that God wanted to send his way. He would have viewed himself as a victim of someone else's machinations and missed his destiny and divine appointments, the places he only dreamed of. He would have never seen his gifts and his passions work together for the kingdom.

> *"For God, said he [Joseph], has made me forget*
> *all my trouble and hardship. . . ."*
> —Genesis 41:51 (AMPC)

Can you forget your toil and hardships, the heartache in your life, and allow God to use them? Can you attempt to put a God-perspective on what He is doing in your life?

Although we each have different tapestries, we all have a destiny that God has placed on our lives, and that tapestry, or our destiny, will intersect to complete the design that God has for us. Throughout Biblical history and personal history, we can see that destiny is often more than we can imagine and so much more than God tells us in advance. I am also aware that we do not know the full extent of the impact our lives have made on others until either later in life or until our descendants begin to see that impact.

We may see a thread the God is weaving and try to unravel the tapestry because we don't really like what is transpiring. However, God will often gently remove our hands from the unraveling process and ask us to resubmit to His will and His purpose. When we again submit ourselves to the process, a beautiful picture will continue to be woven.

When we do not submit to the plan of God and His will, we may cause a detour, deter the process, or thwart our destiny. Something may be woven into our lives that God never intended to be there. It does not mean that God cannot take what has happened—what we may have allowed to happen—and use it for His plan. A true artist can take a mistake in a painting, a tapestry, or a sculpture, incorporate that mistake into the finished product, and make it more beautiful than originally intended. It is often the "mistakes" that give the piece of art the very thing that sets it apart from other pieces and adds value rather than detracting from the value.

|||||||||||||||||||||||||||||||||||||||||||||||||||||||||||||||||||||||||||||||||||||||||

> A true artist can take a mistake in a painting, a tapestry, or a sculpture, incorporate that mistake into the finished product, and make it more beautiful than originally intended.

Isn't that just like our heavenly Father? He takes our mistakes, incorporates them into the finished product, and adds beauty and value to our lives in the process. He does not throw away the unfinished product of our lives, refusing to use us because of a mistake, but He allows us to use the mistake for His glory.

Both Randy and I had first loves before we met one another. His ended during high school, and mine ended immediately after high school. After we married and began our lives together, we both looked back on those relationships and reflected on how God had spared both of us, kept us from making monumental mistakes that could have affected God's destiny for our lives. We knew that God had been merciful to us and continued to place threads of destiny in our lives. Many of us probably have the same or a similar story.

I can remember praying as a young woman that God's plan for my life would align with my plans. Notice that I wanted God to agree with my plan! I did not understand that my prayers should have always been prayed according to His will, not mine. When those prayers were not answered the way I wanted, I was often devastated. My problem was that I did not know the master plan, the picture that God was designing. God always has a plan, a destiny to be fulfilled.

Whenever something happens that we do not expect or plan, it does not mean that God has lost. It simply means that it is different. I am not stating that it is "predestined," that nothing we could have done would have affected the outcome. I am not asserting that it is "karma." I am only expressing that I believe God can take anything that happens and turn it for good. This is Romans 8:28 (NIV) in action:

"And we know that in all things God works for the good of those who love him, who have been called according to his purpose."

Will God's work be fulfilled? Will the picture be completed? Yes, by all means! God will accomplish what He has chosen to do, and it is my job to allow Him to do His will in my life. Regardless of what happens, God is on the throne.

Throughout his life, Randy was highly energetic and competitive, always looking for the next project to do, never satisfied with the status quo, and never willing to stop, slow down, or give up. At the time, I did not understand, but in retrospect, it seems that Randy was on his own timeline, needing to finish what God had placed in his heart, sometimes not even able to articulate what he felt in his spirit that he needed to complete. You see, a person may feel the destiny of God on his life but not be able to understand or express that destiny until it has happened. He or she may know that there is some power that is driving them—that is irresistible—but not know the exact course of events that are yet to unfold. Only God knows what He has determined for you. He has already planned it, and He is weaving it into the tapestry of your life.

"For I know the plans I have for you, declares the Lord. . . ."
—Jeremiah 29:11 (NASB)

". . . [S]o we can do the good things He planned for us long ago."
—Ephesians 2:10 (NLT)

Uncovering Randy's birth circumstances and finding his birth families gave him an added sense of destiny rather than closure. Early in his life when people learned that Randy was adopted, they would ask if he wanted to know his birth family so that he could give himself some sense of closure. He never really needed or wanted "closure" but, instead, felt that there was something more that he needed to know about his adoption. He knew there was a purpose, and it was tied to his destiny.

There were so many things that could have happened pertaining to his birth and adoption that did not happen. When we discussed the outline of this book just three weeks before Randy died, I asked him exactly what he wanted people to know about his story. In just a few short moments, he told me that he wanted to convey the following:

1) He wanted people to know that it does not matter the circumstances of your birth or your upbringing.

2) It does not matter who your adoptive parents may be, who your birth parents may be, or even if you were rejected by them.

3) It does not matter where you were raised or how much influence your family may have wielded.

4) It does not matter how much education you may have, either formal or informal, although you should get as much as possible, read as much as possible, and study every moment that you can.

5) The one thing that needs to get into your spirit is that there is a destiny for your life and that God can and will use you.

|||||||||||||||||||||||||||||||||||||||||||||||||||||||||||||||||||||||||||||||||||||||||

Randy once said, "Purpose is a journey, but destiny is a place. Keep on moving, and don't stop at the place of discouragement. It may look like a good exit to take a rest, but there is nothing at that exit to help you on your journey."

Randy once said, "Purpose is a journey, but destiny is a place. Keep on moving, and don't stop at the place of discouragement.

It may look like a good exit to take a rest, but there is nothing at that exit to help you on your journey." Our journey is just as important as our destiny; there are so many things that God desires for us to learn and experience. You were chosen to do a specific task on your journey to your destiny, to touch the lives of specific people, and to establish a specific thread that must be woven into your tapestry.

Don't stop or become so disappointed on your journey that you cannot fulfill the will of God for your life. Having a sense of destiny and fulfilling that purpose not only give us a goal, an end picture to look toward, but they also help us remember that whenever things go wrong, we can put those things into a different perspective and believe that those events are being woven into the tapestry of our lives. They become learning experiences. Realizing that points us back to a place where although we may not be able to see the entire tapestry, we can know that God is doing SOMETHING through the strings of our lives.

". . . Run with endurance the race God has set before us."
—Hebrews 12:1 (NLT)

The late David Wilkerson once said, "Destiny is what God has predetermined you to be and to become, in His divine will." Randy was not destined to be a businessman, but he was destined to change the world for the cause of Christ, both in spreading the gospel of Jesus Christ and in raising money to facilitate that purpose. God equipped Randy, through purpose, early in life to do the very thing that helped him fulfill his destiny.

It will cost you everything to follow God's path to finding your destiny, but it is your choice to walk into what God has called you to do and be what He has called you to be. Right now, at this moment, God is preparing you for the moment when He directs or redirects you on the path that He has placed before you. Everything that has happened in your life—every experience, your personality bent, your training, your ministry, your life's call—has equipped you to walk in your purpose and fulfill your destiny. The preparation that you are undergoing now is everything you will need to walk into your destiny because God equips those He calls. He provides the loom, the foundation, and the threads for the tapestry. He is constantly tamping down the threads to bring the entire work to a finish.

‖‖

It is not so much your ability that God desires to use to fulfill your destiny but your availability.

It is not so much your ability that God desires to use to fulfill your destiny but your availability. While destiny may be the purpose that God has designed for your life, your destiny is always to do the will of the Father. The purpose that He has planned for you will coincide with how he designed you. God can bring miracles out of what you view as disaster when you learn to embrace your destiny: His will for your life. Finding that destiny will bring energy, fulfillment, and excitement to you!

Just as the tapestry of your life may not yet be finished, God is weaving all of your experiences, your relationships, and your training into His plan for you to fulfill your destiny, the picture that He has designed.

"But I do not account my life of any value nor as precious to myself, if only I may finish my course and the ministry that I received from the Lord Jesus, to testify to the gospel of the grace of God."
—Acts 20:24 (ESV)

"Commit your work to the Lord, and your plans will be established."
—Proverbs 16:3 (ESV)

CONCLUSION

When Randy and I planned the outline for this book, and I began to write it, my idea was that every life is a tapestry of God's grace woven according to God's plan. I never really thought about the fact that one cannot have a life, a tapestry, without it intersecting with another. The picture of one person can never be only about that person's life. By nature, it must intersect with other lives, other people. There are so many threads and so many parts of a life that go together to complete the pre-drawn plan that God has put forth. Randy's life tapestry could have never emerged without the various threads being woven into place. Each of those threads was part of a tapestry, and each will also have its own continuous story. They are intricately designed and woven as part of a whole.

Marion, Parviz, June, Norman, Joel S., everyone who had a significant role in Randy's life was part of the entire tapestry. It didn't end with only those people.

Randy was a son, a husband, a father, a pastor, a mentor, an encourager, a friend, and a believer in people. He poured into the lives of people to help make them better. Randy did not always give the answers, but he helped people look within themselves and their hearts to find the answers that they needed. Although he never rose to the recognized leadership level that he desired, he was a leader of men and women throughout the world. It was only in the last few months of his life that he realized God had him exactly where He wanted him to be, and he was doing exactly what God wanted him to do: mentoring, training, and equipping the next generation of leaders.

God chose Randy to do a specific work just as He chooses us all. Randy had a choice as to whether or not he would be used by God to change the world. He chose to live within God's best for his life. Randy's genetic history, his spiritual roots, and everything that made Randy who he was could only be as important as his availability to be used. Throughout the course of our time in Griffin, Georgia, Randy's theme for the ministry was, "One church can change the world." Randy chose to allow God to place threads of his life in a tapestry that would help change the world. We're all given that same choice: surrender to the plan of God for our lives, or resist it. If we surrender, there is no limit to what God can do in us and through us.

IIIIIIIIIIIIIIIIIIIIIIIIIIIIIIIIIIIIIIIIIIIIIIIIIIIIIIIIIIIIIIIIIIIIIIIIIIIIIIIIIII

Randy chose to allow God to place threads of his life in a tapestry that would help change the world.

From the very beginning of Randy's life, there was a destiny that begged to be fulfilled. He did not realize that his destiny had been fulfilled before he died, and since then, I have often wondered if any of us will ever realize that our own destinies have been completely fulfilled. Of course, there is more Randy could have done and many plans that were already in place for him to complete. In looking back over his life, Randy's work ethic, his passion for God, and his own teachability set the tone for his destiny to be fulfilled.

On October 31, 2019, Randy suddenly passed away due to complications from surgery. We had no idea that death was imminent. He lived life to the fullest up until the day he died, entertaining all who visited his hospital room with ideas of what he would eat as soon as he was given the freedom to do so. He laughed and joked about his pain, telling his friends that women were much tougher than men!

The last sermon Randy preached was a missions sermon imploring people to give to the kingdom of God so that we could build bigger lifeboats for those who have never heard the gospel of Jesus Christ. His passion for winning the lost was palpable during that last sermon. He never gave up searching for ways to spread the gospel. He never quit telling others or living to tell others about what salvation could do for each person. He died on the last day of the month of our mission emphasis. He delivered his heart in that last sermon, and it continues to serve as a reminder that we are not yet finished. In my home today, hangs a painting of a lifeboat that shows all who enter the importance I still place on building a bigger lifeboat.

Although Randy's life on earth has ended, the tapestry has not been finished. There is more to this story. People were affected by and woven into his life, and they will continue the work as God keeps weaving.

||||||||||||||||||||||||||||||||||||||||||||||||||||||||||||||||||||||||||||||||||||

Although Randy's life on earth has
ended, the tapestry has not been
finished. There is more to this story.
People were affected by and woven
into his life, and they will continue
the work as God keeps weaving.

Randy attended Goose Creek High School just outside of
Charleston, South Carolina. In his high school years and while playing
football, he was mentored by a football coach who later left teaching
to become a minister. Randy attended a youth camp where he truly
submitted to the call of God on his life. His senior pastor, Rev. Fred
Richards, helped strengthen that call as Randy grew into a stalwart
man of God who would not back down or turn from what he knew
was right. These events and these men were woven into his life during
moments that affected the rest of his life. They were threads of destiny
that ultimately helped complete the picture that God was weaving.

Randy was a youth pastor in Oxford, Florida, and in Springdale,
Arkansas. He was a senior pastor in Toccoa, Georgia, and in Griffin,
Georgia. During his time at all these churches, Randy mentored and
poured himself into the lives of many men, women, boys, and girls
and became a part of the tapestry of their lives. I do not know the
number of people who were called into full-time ministry or those
who went into marketplace ministry as a result of being mentored
by Randy. I cannot count the number of souls who heard and will
continue to hear the gospel of Jesus Christ or those who made a

commitment to follow Christ at Randy's invitation. I cannot count the amount of money that was raised to further spread the good news of Jesus Christ. However, I DO know that the number of people who listened to Randy's story and were impacted by his ministry and life is vast. Randy became a part of their tapestry and their destiny.

God always has a pre-drawn plan, a purpose for everything that He allows to happen in our lives. Regardless of the thread that is being pulled through the loom right now, there is an ultimate plan for your tapestry. You may not know what God is weaving. You may be a thread in the tapestry of someone else. Just know that He is weaving a masterpiece. Let your life count for something. Use what God has given you and what He has put into your life. Develop what He has given you, so it can be used for the glory of God. It does not matter if you are now a thread or if you are the entire tapestry. You are still important in the plan of God. You are part of God's master plan, a picture of destiny.

"For the vision is yet for the appointed [future] time, It hurries toward the goal [of fulfillment]; it will not fail. Even though it delays, wait [patiently] for it, Because it will certainly come; it will not delay."
—Habakkuk 2:3 (AMP)

As Randy's widow, I have found that although death may separate us, it will never defeat us. I know there is more for me to do, more for our children to continue, and more that God has planned. There is a legacy to be lived. When this tapestry is finished will depend on what God's pre-drawn plan has been. He has not yet revealed it to me, and I don't know that He will. I do know that one day, either on this earth or in the next world, I may be allowed to look back, see a lovely picture, and say, "Oh, that's what this was all about!"

That is significant.